Train Wreck!

Ashtabula, Ohio (see Chapter 7)

Train Wreck!

By WESLEY S. GRISWOLD

Illustrated with contemporary engravings and photographs

The Stephen Greene Press
BRATTLEBORO, VERMONT · 1969

Designed by R. L. Dothard Associates, printed by The Vermont
Printing Company, and bound by The Book Press.
Library of Congress catalog card number: 72-88771
Standard Book Number: 8289-0099-X

Bibliography and Acknowledgments

For facts and local color throughout the writing of this book, I have relied almost exclusively on reports published in contemporary newspapers, and on the inquest and investigation transcripts printed in those same newspapers. My chief source has been the New York *Times*, whose long, distinguished existence parallels nearly all of U.S. railroading history. In addition, I found helpful material in the Boston *Evening Transcript, Herald,* and *Journal;* the Buffalo *Express;* the Burlington (Vt.) *Free Press & Times;* the Chicago *Examiner, Herald & Examiner,* and *Tribune;* the Cleveland *Herald* and *Leader;* the *Engineering News* and *American Contract Journal;* the Los Angeles *Times;* the New York *Journal of Commerce;* the Philadelphia *Public Ledger;* the San Francisco *Call* and *Chronicle;* the Springfield (Mass.) *Union;* and, by no means least in interest and thoroughness of coverage, the Windsor (Vt.) *Vermont Journal.*

I also drew upon the following books for additional information or confirmation:

ADAMS, JOHN QUINCY, *Memoirs: Comprising Portions of His Diary from 1795 to 1849.* Charles Francis Adams, editor, Vol. 9. Philadelphia, J. B. Lippincott & Co., 1876.

ALEXANDER, E. P., *Iron Horses: American Locomotives 1829–1900.* New York, Bonanza Books, 1941.

HOLBROOK, STEWART H., *The Story of American Railroads.* New York, Crown Publishers, 1947.

HUNGERFORD, EDWARD, *Men and Iron: A History of New York Central.* New York, Thomas Y. Crowell Co., 1938.

LANE, WHEATON J., *From Indian Trail to Iron Horse: Travel and Transportation in New Jersey, 1620–1860.* Princeton, N. J., Princeton University Press, 1939.

McCREADY, ALBERT L., *Railroads in the Days of Steam.* New York, American Heritage Publishing Co., Inc., 1960.

MENCKEN, AUGUST, *The Railroad Passenger Car: An Illustrated History of the First Hundred Years with Accounts by Contemporary Passengers.* Baltimore, the Johns Hopkins Press, 1957.

SHAW, ROBERT B., *Down Brakes: A History of Railroad Accidents, Safety Precautions and Operating Practices in the United States of America.* London, Geneva, P. R. Macmillan, Ltd., 1961. (It is regrettable that this excellent, practically encyclopedic book is already out of print and very difficult to find. I am grateful for the loan of a copy from Richard Sanders Allen.)

STOVER, JOHN F., *American Railroads*. Chicago and London, the University of Chicago Press, 1961.

To Stephen Greene I am indebted for the suggestion that I write this book, and to Janet Greene for wise and constructive editorial assistance in carrying out her husband's suggestion. I would like also to express my appreciation for technical information given me by C. M. Bishop, Signal & Train Control Branch, United States Department of Transportation. I am most grateful for the valuable advice and candid reactions of my old friends Frank Rowsome and Anne and Brooke Whiting, and those of my parents, Marjorie and Arthur Griswold. To R. H. Kindig, Don Bloch, Carl M. Davidson, John Wilhelm, Kathleen Pierson, Bernard J. Kelly, Warren A. Reeder, Jr., and Linda McC. Burrows I owe cordial thanks for help in tracking down elusive photographs. Lastly, I am happy to acknowledge my debt to the Research Library, University of California, Los Angeles; the Los Angeles Public Library; and the Henry E. Huntington Library, San Marino, California, for the richness of their collections and the unstinting helpfulness of their staffs.

W. S. G.

Harper's Weekly *of February 19, 1887, aroused by the Vermont disaster renewed the publishing community's crusade against the use of coal stoves and kerosene lamps in railroad cars by printing this symbolic drawing of the victims in the appalling wreck at the White River Bridge near West Hartford. (See Chapter 9.)*

Contents

(RR, locations & dates of wrecks)

1

When the Going Was Rough
(November 8, 1833-September 15, 1958)

BLESSED, *ever blessed be the name of God, that I am alive and have escaped unhurt from the most dreadful catastrophe that ever my eyes beheld!*

So, in an untypical burst of emotion, did former President John Quincy Adams begin his diary entry for November 8, 1833. On the morning of that day, he and Cornelius Vanderbilt, along with several dozen others, had been involved in the first significant U.S. train wreck. Rocking across New Jersey on the little two-year-old Camden & Amboy Railroad, in primitive cars that Adams said were like large stagecoaches, this cargo of trustful early railroad travelers had come a cropper when burning lubrication in an axle housing caused the axle to break and the train to leave the track. Here were perhaps the first American victims of that enduring nemesis of railroadmen, the "hotbox."

Seven weeks earlier, a stray hog had derailed the C&A's original steam engine, the British-built *John Bull*, a vehicle with chimney-like stack, a whiskey barrel for a water tank, and leather water pipes stitched together by a Bordentown shoemaker. Upon colliding with the hog, "the locomotive was thrown off and plunged with its head in the gutter," a local newspaper reported. At the time, the *John Bull* was pulling the first C&A passenger train to be drawn by a locomotive instead of by two horses in tandem harness. Nobody had been hurt but the hog, which was instantly killed, and a nervous man who somersaulted out an open car window in an uncalled-for effort of self-preservation. On the morning of November 8th, a much more destructive accident occurred not far from the spot where the hog had met its fate. It was the earliest American railroad wreck in which passengers were killed.

Adams, then sixty-six years old and about to begin the second term of his post-Presidential career as a Massachusetts Congressman, was not injured. Vanderbilt, thirty-nine, was seriously hurt, though the precise nature of his injuries remains in some doubt. One account states that the Captain, as he was then called, suffered broken ribs and a punctured lung, injuries from which he nearly died. Adams, who had the opportunity to see for himself, and was ever governed by a lawyer's sober regard for facts, reported that "Captain Vanderbilt had his leg broken."

Whatever Vanderbilt's physical damage was, his experience left him with a traumatic distrust of railroads that was not overcome for nearly three decades afterward. In his own good time, the future Commodore would conclude that he had been missing a prime opportunity for enrichment, and be moved to remedy his error by piecing together the New York Central network.

The trip that Adams and Vanderbilt shared on that November day in 1833 began spiritedly. The train's engineer, under orders never to exceed a speed of 20 miles per hour, was disobeying regulations in order to make up lost time. Another employee of the railroad normally rode along on every trip expressly to keep tabs on the engineer's speed, but on this day he was absent.

"Of the first ten miles," Adams recorded in his diary that evening, "two were run in four minutes, marked by a watch of a Mr. De Yong, in the same car and division [compartment] with me. They stopped, oiled the wheels, and proceeded. We had gone about five miles further, and had traversed one mile in one minute and thirty-six seconds, when the front left wheel of the car in which I was, having taken fire and burned for several minutes, slipped off the rail."

Adams's coach tilted alarmingly to the left, but was then hauled back up onto the track by the increasing pull of the car behind it, which had lurched to the right at the moment of derailment. The second coach kept leaning farther over until it was skidding along the ground on its right side.

"The train was stopped," wrote Adams, "I suppose within five seconds of the time when our wheel slipped off the rail, but it was then going at the rate of sixty feet in a second, and the overturned car dragged nearly two hundred feet before it could stop." The train might have been stopped sooner if it had had the services of its two brakemen. Instead, one of these men had been riding on the roof of the car that overturned, and he was thrown into the adjacent shrubbery; the other was back on the luggage car at the end of the train, trying to put out a blaze in a bale of cotton that

Lurid but realistic scenes like this conception of the moment of collision in a "cornfield meet" of two passenger trains of the 1880's helped stir public demand and instigate legislative action to make U. S. railroading safer.

had been ignited by sparks flying from the engine. "Of sixteen persons in two of the three compartments of the car that overset," Adams went on, "only one escaped unhurt. . . . One side of the car was stove in, and almost demolished. One man . . . was so dreadfully mangled that he died within ten minutes; another . . . can probably not survive the day." He didn't.

"The scene of sufferance was excruciating," Adams continued. "Men, women, and a child scattered along the road, bleeding, mangled, groaning, writhing in torture, and dying, was a trial of feeling to which I had never before been called; and when the thought came over me that a few yards more of pressure on the car in which I was would have laid me a prostrate corpse like him who was before my eyes, or a cripple for life; and, more insupportable still, what if my wife and grandchild had been in the car behind me! Merciful God! . . ."

Similar scenes and similar sentiments became almost commonplace in some of the dangerous years that followed, when railroads provided the only means of rapid transportation and nearly every factor militated against their safety. The men who built the roads were so anxious to lay track and start trains running over it that they paid scant attention to maintaining either roadbed or rolling stock (both in degrees of neglect again today). The men who operated the trains were far more inclined to bravado than caution. Bridges weren't strong enough to bear the ever increasing loads that rolled across them. Brakes for long were applied by hand, and were pitifully inadequate. Cars were made of wood, heated by stoves, and lighted by kerosene or other inflammables. When wrecked in cold weather, they almost invariably caught fire and burned to cinders. Trackside signals were crude, easily misinterpreted, and often ignored. Railroads were slow to take advantage of the telegraph for even the beginnings of reliable traffic control.

Oddly enough, the public, excited by its new-found ability to outspeed the horse, at first tended to admire the rash, competitive attitude of early, youthful train crews toward their tasks and responsibilities. An English visitor to the United States, Charles Richard Weld, commented in bewilderment and exasperation on a wreck he experienced while traveling by rail from Cumberland, Maryland, to Washington, D. C., in 1855:

> In vain was the conductor urged to slacken the excessive speed [he wrote]. With blind if not wilful recklessness it was maintained, and at length . . . a terrific crash and a series of dislocatory heavings and collisions, terminating in deathlike silence and the overthrow of the car which we occupied, gave certain evidence that we had gone off the line.
>
> I have no distinct recollection how I crawled out of the car, for I was half stunned, but I remember being highly delighted when I found my limbs sound. On looking around, the spectacle was extraordinary. With the exception of about half the middle car and engine there was scarcely a portion of the train that was not more or less broken. The wheels were whirled to great distances and the rails for the length of many yards either wholly wrenched from the sleepers or converted into snake-heads [up-bent strips of jagged iron].
>
> When I saw the state of things I was extremely indignant, for by the wilful conduct of the conductor our lives had been placed in imminent peril, but when I spoke in strong terms of him to my fellow passengers, urging that we ought to report him to the directors of the line, I found my feelings were not only unshared but all rather approved than otherwise his exertions to get us in on time.

Each new safety appliance introduced on railroads in the 19th Century was hailed as a panacea by a public and press desperately anxious to reduce the high accident rate. With this front-page drawing, Frank Leslie's Illustrated Newspaper of January 28, 1882, paid tribute to the "torpedo alarm" placed on rails to warn of an unexpectedly halted train ahead. With the new device, the editor assured his readers, "collisions may easily be prevented." At least it helped.

Accidents on railways are thought so light of in America [the ruffled Englishman concluded] it is useless to remonstrate.

This permissive attitude on the part of American railroad travelers changed abruptly before the end of the 1850's. By that time heavier, faster trains were in common use, carrying increased numbers of passengers, and these trains were beginning to have accidents that resulted in the deaths of dozens of persons and grave injuries to scores more.

Some of these accidents, described in the chapters that follow, were outstanding shockers that stirred public opinion to demand remedial action—though it came at glacial speed. A few of the wrecks became known to an outraged nation by their place names alone—Camp Hill, Angola, Ashtabula, Revere, Chatsworth. They served as horrible examples for every advocate of improved protection to cite in his missionary efforts to obtain stricter, stronger regulations. They were the chief stimuli to the inventors of safety devices, the devisers of more provident operating procedures.

Even a casual scrutiny of the history of railroading in this country reveals wide time-lags, however, between the introduction and general acceptance of protective improvements. The average gap stretches at least twenty-five years. Although most of us are well aware that railroad travel in the course of time became admittedly the safest form of mass transportation in the United States, one is left marveling at the fact that it was able to do so.

This book's backward looks at some outstanding wrecks of one hundred and twenty-five years of American railroading—nearly the entire span of its history to date—remind us that many of them happened because of human failure, which has survived the most ingenious efforts to anticipate or prevent it. That familiar troublemaker, one cannot help remarking in a day when efforts are being made to revive faltering railroad passenger service by speeding it up, can precipitate an accident as readily at 120 mph as at 60, and with predictably far more direful results.

Also detectable in the accounts of past disasters in the succeeding pages is an occasional ironic tendency of history almost to repeat itself, as if progress had never taken place. Precisely the same kind of accident, for example, that John Quincy Adams reported in 1833 was responsible for wrecking the *Congressional Limited* ninety years later. Exactly the same sort of disaster that happened at the South Norwalk drawbridge in 1853 occurred again, though we'll never know why, one hundred and five years later at the entrance to Newark Bay.

It has been pointed out elsewhere that disasters on steamboats, particularly in earlier days, and on airliners have often outstripped in dimensions the worst railroad wreck that ever happened, but that they almost always have occurred in remote places or have produced no survivors at all. In consequence, they have failed to provide the rich lode of human interest inherent in stories of railroad wrecks, in which most adults who have ever traveled anywhere can feel a vicarious sense of involvement.

Passenger-train accidents have usually taken place within easy reach of the morbidly curious and have invariably produced voluble survivors, whose firsthand accounts, together with those of awed bystanders who watched the wrecks occur, have made fascinating reading. They still do. It was because of that fact, as well as with an impulse to contribute to the historical record of American railway travel in the apparent twilight of its existence, that the author has reconstructed from original newspaper coverage the stories of the memorable passenger-train accidents that follow.

2

Headlong into the River
(South Norwalk, Connecticut: May 6, 1853)

A RUMOR swept through the newspaper offices of New York City around noon on May 6, 1853, that the good Dr. Oliver Wendell Holmes had been killed in a train wreck that had occurred two hours earlier at South Norwalk, Connecticut. A few of the more scholarly reporters were promptly set to work scribbling obituaries of the "witty poet and eminent surgeon" of Harvard, whose eloquent tribute to Old Ironsides had already been drummed into the resistant memories of a generation of American schoolboys.

The rumor, happily, soon proved to be false, like many an other report reaching the metropolis from the scene of the accident on the New York & New Haven Railroad that dewy morning. Five doctors indeed had died in the disaster, and fifteen others had suffered injuries of varying seriousness, but Dr. Holmes was not among them. What was clear almost from the first alarm, however, was that the wreck had been an extraordinarily bad one, by far the worst that had occurred in the United States since the beginning of railway travel more than twenty years earlier. The death toll of this accident was forty-six lives, more than twice as many as were lost in any previous one. The injured, though, numbered less than half as many as the dead. Ordinarily, the ratio was reversed, but this was not an ordinary accident in any respect. The fact that the ruined train had been exceptionally freighted with members of the medical profession was only one of its curious aspects.

Thirty doctors had climbed aboard the 8:00 A.M. express for New Haven, Hartford, Springfield, Worcester, and Boston that Friday morning. They had been attending a week-long convention of the American Medical Association in New York City. At least half of them survived the subsequent wreck in condition to provide swifter succor than was generally available after an accident. Even such quick relief did not come fast enough for the majority of victims, however. Most of them, in a very few minutes, had drowned. The express had plunged through an open drawbridge, which the engineer had failed to notice until just a few seconds before his train reached it. That was time enough to enable the engineer, the fireman, and the brakemen of the first four cars to leap to the ground, but not enough for any of the passengers to do so. They remained unaware of their peril until they found themselves flying through the air or submerged in the Norwalk River, many of them hopelessly pinned under debris.

In the Connecticut General Assembly next morning, Representative Smith of Sharon rose and shouted at his colleagues: "I will not call it accident; I denounce it as wholesale, bloody, murderous massacre. In my opinion, the wretch whose brutal heedlessness or ignorance caused it should be hung on a gibbet higher than Haman's, and exposed to the scorn and execration of outraged humanity." Smith's reaction was widely shared.

So severely hurt was the engineer, Edward W. Tucker, after jumping from his locomotive cab, that he was said to be dying. From a bed in a compassionate stranger's house in Norwalk, Tucker swore to the inquest jurors that just before the accident he had clearly seen the signal indicating that the bridge was closed and all was well. He insisted that he couldn't have been mistaken. The signal was a bright red ball, two feet in diameter, which dangled most of the time from a crossbar at the top of a forty-foot pole mounted on the draw of the bridge. When the bridge was to be opened for a boat to pass, the bridge-tender hauled down the ball, laid it on a bridge beam, and started the steam machinery that swung the sixty-foot span of the draw crossways to the railroad tracks. He did not hoist the ball back up to the top of the pole on its pulley chain until he had closed the bridge once more. At night, the ball contained a light.

On the morning of the calamity at South Norwalk, the bridge-tender had lowered the ball and opened the bridge fully fifteen minutes before the express came along from the southwest. The little steamer *Pacific* had just churned through the gap and was thirty or forty yards beyond the bridge when the train was heard approaching. There had not been time to close the bridge, and the red ball was still down. At least a dozen eyewitnesses, on land or in boats, later swore to that fact. Engineer Tucker was miserably alone in his repeated insistence that he had seen the ball

This is how an artist for the *New York Illustrated News* visualized the train wreck at South Norwalk, Connecticut, on the morning of May 6, 1853. The smokestack beyond the passenger car ripped in two is that of the steamer Pacific, which had just passed down the Norwalk River on its way to Long Island Sound. The bare signal pole on top of the bridge should have warned the engineer of the train that the draw was open.

riding at the top of the pole a minute or two before the wreck.

At eight o'clock that morning, the New Haven express had left Canal Street station, at the southern end of Manhattan Island. It then comprised, in addition to locomotive and tender, two baggage cars, the second of which contained a small smoking compartment, and four passenger cars. At the Twenty-seventh Street station of the line, the train took on a fifth passenger car. Since this was an express, it was scheduled to stop at Stamford and at Bridgeport but not at Norwalk, which is situated between them, close to Long Island Sound. Norwalk station, to the frequent confusion of newspapermen reporting the accident that ensued, was located in South Norwalk, a thousand feet west of the drawbridge, which placed it closer to New York than the bridge, and two miles away from Norwalk. Local trains all stopped at Norwalk station. None of the expresses did.

Engineers of trains bound for New York, approaching the South Norwalk drawbridge from the east, had a fine view of the red-ball signal for at least a half-mile before they reached the Norwalk River. The engineer of an upbound train could first see the signal three-quarters of a mile away, before passing Norwalk station, but trees and buildings occasionally hid it from his sight thereafter, while the train rounded an abrupt curve, until he was within 550 feet of the bridge. From that point on, the signal pole was in full view.

No upbound local would have difficulty stopping in time to avoid trouble even if the drawbridge happened to be open, though only 1,086 feet of track lay between Norwalk station and the bridge. In that short distance, whether or not the engineer had paid attention to the position of the red ball, his train, barely under way, could easily be braked to a stop at first sight of the open draw.

This was decidedly not true for expresses, which were accustomed to average 30 mph between stops. Edward Tucker, driving the eight o'clock express on May 6th, had been given only one verbal instruction by the conductor when they started out that morning: "Watch out for the red ball at the Norwalk bridge." This vital order, he failed to heed.

Tucker was in a most unusual situation. Although he had begun driving trains for the New Haven road almost as soon as it commenced operations in 1849, he had not piloted an engine over the line between New York and New Haven since January

1851. On that last previous occasion, he had been involved in a head-on collision near Mamaroneck, in which he had been extensively injured. He was absolved of responsibility for the crash. The conductor was obviously to blame, for he had ordered Tucker to proceed toward New Haven on a single track when a down train was expected. Tucker had strongly protested the order, but the conductor had persuaded him to proceed by saying that he had sent a message ahead and there was nothing to worry about. The conductor was wrong. Tucker was hurt badly enough in the resulting collision to need several months of recuperation.

The company benignly paid him a year's wages, and he set off for California to try his luck in the waning Gold Rush. Fortune failed to smile on him there, though, and by March 1853 he was back in New Haven, applying for his old job with the railroad. A new superintendent hired him, but as a relief engineer, which meant that he made no regular runs. This occasion on the morning of May 6th was the first time in more than two years that he had been scheduled to drive a train from New York to New Haven. If misgivings weighed on his mind because of this fact, no evidence of them appeared in the subsequent inquest testimony. "I am as familiar with the road as I am with my ABC's," he assured the jurors. But a man can forget a lot about a route in two years of absence.

The trip went smoothly, at least, as far as South Norwalk. The express rolled past Norwalk station at a speed that Tucker afterward estimated at from 10 to 12 mph, but passengers and onlookers variously judged to have been between 35 and 50. All were doubtless mistaken. After every railroad accident, train crews almost invariably underestimate the speed that preceded the wreck; passengers almost as consistently overestimate it. This does not mean that any of them deliberately lie; it is mostly a matter of point of view and experience, and, of course, defensiveness on the part of the train crew. Until the invention of the automatically recording speedometer for locomotives, investigators of railroad wrecks were customarily obliged to conclude that the true speed lay somewhere between the professional and nonprofessional estimates.

That is what they did after the wreck at South Norwalk. The train, they said, approached the bridge "at the rate of not less than twenty miles per hour, and obviously without any regard to the condition of the bridge." When the engine was only 369 feet from the open draw, Tucker suddenly realized the danger. He sounded the two short, sharp blasts of the whistle that were the universal signal to brakemen to apply the hand brakes.

This time, brakemen in the forward cars did not even try to obey the "Down brakes" signal; they jumped off the train, one of them because he said he saw the engineer and fireman do so. As a consequence, the train kept on going, its speed unchecked. Eleven seconds later the engine fell into the Norwalk River, dragging several cars after it.

Brakemen in the last three cars did man their brakes, however. As a result, though the tracks were still slippery with dew, enough drag was applied to the rear of the train to force the last two passenger cars to a stop before they reached the gap in the track, and to cause the car ahead of them to rip apart in the middle. Locomotive, tender, baggage cars, the first two passenger cars and the front end of the third, hurtled headlong into the river, which was at high tide, and thus nine to twelve feet deep. The river's bed was a deep layer of ooze, and into this the locomotive, after leaping the 60-foot gap and smashing against the center pier of the bridge, immediately sank out of sight. The tender somersaulted and landed upside down on the sunken engine. The first baggage car struck the center pier and burst apart. The second baggage car, with eight shocked smokers in it, flew sideways and fell beneath the north end of the draw. It landed against piling, which partially held it up, and it did not sink. The first passenger car dropped and disappeared, crushed by the weight of the second, which fell on top of it, along with the front end of the third.

A resident of Norwalk who was within a hundred yards of the bridge when the wreck occurred saw the entire catastrophe unfold. "The third passenger car snapped like a match," he said, "the flooring, the sides, and the foremost end flying forward, with a jerk, half across the draw. Many of the seats and the dislodged window sashes, with a crowd of timber fragments, were impelled, some of them, fully across the gulf, and two of the passengers, who were seated just at the spot where the car snapped asunder, were thrown full twenty feet forward and pitched with frightful force upon the ruins of the second and first cars."

This dumfounded witness ran forward to the edge of the gap. "I heard the crash of breaking timbers," he wrote later that day, "and one scream, uttered simultaneously by many voices. Then, for a second or two, all was still as death. Then I heard the gurgling of the waters as they rushed into the cars, forming eddies or little whirlpools on the surface. In another moment, shrieks from those in the rear cars and in the hind part of the third passenger car filled the air, and in the next instant there was but one scene of indescribable confusion."

Thomas Hicks, a rising young portrait painter from New York City, elected to the National Academy two years before at the age of twenty-eight, had been riding in the second passenger car with a woman friend whom the newspapers identified only as "Miss King." They had been seated on the right-hand side of the car, four rows from the rear, when the accident happened. Theirs was among the most remarkable experiences recorded.

"Without warning or intimation of any kind," Hicks declared, "I beheld the front part of the car rushing toward me in fragments, the passengers being tossed in the air like chaff, dashed up against the top of the car, and thrown about in a hurricane of destruction."

Almost simultaneously he found himself pushed down by a mass of wreckage, Miss King gone, and the car rapidly filling with water. He crawled out from under the weight of debris and began frantically feeling around under the black water in an effort to locate his companion. When the water reached his chin, however, he felt impelled to seek an escape route. It wasn't hard to find. The roof had split lengthwise when this car fell upon the one beneath it. Hicks climbed out through the gaping crack above him. For a moment more, he clung to the splintered roof, peering below in a final attempt to discern Miss King.

Rescuers were now beginning to arrive in small boats from the shore and from the *Pacific*, which had put back to help. One of them called to Hicks and asked him whom he was looking for. When the artist described how Miss King had been dressed, his questioner astonished and gratified him by declaring that he had just seen a young lady dressed like that climb up to the tracks. Hicks stepped into the man's boat and was rowed ashore, where Miss King rushed out of the gathering crowd to give him an emotional welcome. She excitedly explained that when the car's roof split wide, she was somehow tossed out through the opening, without having any idea how. Although she had been cut about the face, she had not got wet at all. She added, with justified pride, that, while she was in the course of recovering her wits, she saw a man's arm reach out of the floating wreckage beside her. She had pushed the debris aside and hauled him to the surface and to safety. Miss King had evidently not spent much time, if any, hunting for Mr. Hicks.

The rescue forces were armed with axes, and began hacking away at the car frames in hope of releasing passengers trapped beneath them. There had been more than a hundred people in the first four cars. Nearly half of them, mostly in the forward passenger car, had been killed. All eight smokers in the second baggage car had escaped without help.

A Hartford doctor had been among the first of the unharmed physicians aboard to begin treating the injured, for he had been seated just back of the center of the third passenger car. When that car was pulled apart, the floor broke off right at his feet, and he was left staring down upon the scene of disaster from a front-row seat. He and others from the rear cars of the train scrambled out and began rescue work at once.

No coroner could be found promptly, so a Norwalk justice of the peace empaneled a local jury of inquest. It began hearing testimony from survivors in the afternoon of the same day. Several of the survivors were injured, some of them seriously, and had been carried to homes near the scene of the wreck. The jurors moved from house to house that afternoon, obtaining their stories of what had happened and how it had happened.

Engineer Tucker's fireman, George Elmer, had not been injured when he jumped from the train. Nor had he been aware of the position of the signal. "It is not my duty to look for it," he said. He told the jurors that he had never fired for Tucker before this trip, but that Tucker was certainly unlike other New Haven Railroad engineers he had worked with, in that he hadn't read a newspaper at any time while the train was moving. This startling revelation about the casual attitude of other engineers of the road made a deep impression on the jurors, and on a special committee of the Connecticut legislature, whose members arrived to conduct their own investigation of the accident at the beginning of the following week. It also disturbed some members of the public, and inspired one writer to a newspaper to suggest that thereafter a special watchman, "duly deprived of newspapers, books, and the bottle," be employed on every railroad train to sit in the cab of the locomotive along with the engineer and fireman, "with no duty except to be eternally vigilant."

A damaging rumor was spread very shortly after the accident, to the effect that because the 8:00 A.M. express was running eight minutes behind schedule, the conductor had told the engineer to "go through Norwalk like hell." This was found to be wholly without basis and was specifically denied in the inquest jury's verdict, delivered on Tuesday, May 10th.

The jurors found Tucker guilty of gross negligence in not having discovered that the red ball was down: "In running around the curve [just west of the drawbridge] at such a rapid rate, and under such circumstances, we think him guilty of the most criminal recklessness.

"At the same time," the jurors concluded, in a fair-minded way, "we do not think the entire responsibility of this disaster rests upon him."

It proceeded then to censure the railroad's chief officials for knowingly permitting most trains to approach the South Norwalk drawbridge at speeds of 20 mph or more, when the company's own rule book stated that "all trains must run with care in approaching Norwalk River Bridge."

The jury further declared that conductors ought to be given greater responsibility for the safe operation of trains, since they were in charge of them; that when they weren't busy punching tickets, they should keep a sharp lookout for signals; and that Conductor Charles Comstock, of the train that was wrecked, should have told the engineer he was going too fast for safety as he drew near Norwalk River. Comstock had been chatting with one of the brakemen at that time.

The inquest jury at Norwalk found more things wrong with the New York & New Haven Railroad than pertained specifically to the wreck at South Norwalk. Their recital of its shortcomings doubtless would have applied almost equally well to nearly every railroad in the land in 1853. "The public demand a rate of speed which on the road as originally constructed can scarcely be run with safety," its verdict commented. "The road was constructed too cheaply to warrant the highest rate of speed—the grades are too heavy, the curves of too small radius, and the bridges are not of as permanent a character as they should be."

Three members of Connecticut's House of Representatives and one member of the state Senate conducted an independent inquiry into the causes of the New Haven Railroad wreck of May

6th. They reached conclusions almost identical to those of the inquest jury, and found that "the weight of responsibility for the calamity must rest on the Company."

The most important result of these investigations was that a bill was soon introduced in the Connecticut legislature that established the state's first Board of Railroad Commissioners, who were to look into all complaints of unsafe conditions or unwise practices on Connecticut railroads, investigate within twenty-four hours every railroad accident that involved loss of human life, and propose legislative action to correct abuses and improve railway safety. As the bill was drawn, it would have given the Board of Railroad Commissioners arbitrary powers to enforce their rulings, and even halt operations on any line that failed to comply. The General Assembly proceeded to water down the bill until the board was left with only the power to give advice and recommend remedies for unsafe conditions or practices. The establishment of the board was in itself, however, a large step forward toward safer travel on railroads. Other states soon followed suit.

Meanwhile, the New York & New Haven Railroad had put into practice a suggestion first embodied in the draft of the new law: All their trains now were ordered to come to a full stop before crossing any drawbridge. This, one of the company officials explained, was a concession to public feelings.

And was the traveling public duly grateful for this safety measure? Not at all, reported the New York *Journal of Commerce* a few days later. Passengers were already grumbling at being "unnecessarily" delayed in their journeys.

3

The Picnic That Never Was
(Camp Hill, Pennsylvania: July 17, 1856)

A N ominous shadow hurrying across a grassy bank gave Engineer William Lee first warning that a collision was imminent. The bank, marking the west end of a blind curve, rose only a couple of hundred yards ahead of his slowly moving locomotive, *Aramingo*. The long shadow crossing the far slope of the curve was that of an approaching engine, smoke streaming from its stack, its features distorted by the low rays of the rising sun behind it.

Aramingo was hauling the first regularly scheduled train of the day down the single track of the North Pennsylvania Railroad from Gwynedd to Philadelphia on the hot morning of July 17, 1856. It was a short, mixed train, taking on a few passengers and cans of milk at frequent stops. There were now twenty-four persons aboard, including the train crew.

At the shocking sight of the shadow, Engineer Lee, yanking back the throttle, yelled to his fireman, "Here they come!" Both men had been aware that an upbound excursion train was past due. Lee had tried to persuade the conductor, his superior, to wait for it at the previous station, Fort Washington, but had failed. The conductor was convinced that the excursion train was waiting for them on the next siding, three stops ahead.

In quick succession, Lee shut off steam, reversed the engine, and twice blew the two-blast whistle signal "Down brakes!" The fireman leapt to comply, and, on the cars behind, so did the conductor and brakeman.

Already the oncoming locomotive, drawing a long string of passenger cars, had burst out of the curve and was bearing down upon them at a fast rate.

"I jumped back to the tank and held on to the reversing lever," Lee later told a coroner's jury. His agonized hope that the other train would be able to stop before hitting his own was all too obviously forlorn. The fireman jumped off. Lee, with

Aramingo nearly at a standstill, waited until the gap between the two locomotives had narrowed to about thirty feet. The approaching train was "still coming very rapidly—at least twenty-five to thirty miles an hour." Then Lee jumped, running and tumbling down the railroad embankment.

In the shattering crash that almost instantly followed, the oncoming engine climbed the face of *Aramingo*, splitting that locomotive apart and knocking it over on one side. The assaulting engine then fell backward upon the first car of its own train, crushing that and showering it and the two following cars with flaming embers from its gutted firebox. The splintered wooden frames of the cars had already been doused with kerosene from smashed lamps. They quickly caught fire. Screams rose from injured passengers pinned beneath the blazing wreckage, and from those struggling with one another to escape the flames.

An hour and a half earlier, when the sky was barely light, a happy, noisy throng of youngsters, escorted by adult relatives and a few priests, had gathered at Philadelphia's Master Street station to board a North Pennsylvania Railroad excursion train. They were pupils of the Sunday school of St. Michael's Roman Catholic Church in Kensington, a district of the city populated largely by immigrant Irish. This was the day chosen for their annual picnic. The site selected was Fort Washington, fourteen and a half miles northwest of Philadelphia, where there were pleasant rural campgrounds.

Sixteen hundred tickets for the outing had been sold, and the little NPRR had arranged to provide two ten-car special trains to take the picnickers to Fort Washington and back. The first excursion train was scheduled to leave Market Street station at 5 A.M., the second at 8.

By five o'clock, several hundred persons had found seats for themselves in the nine passenger cars of "Excursion No. 1," as the railroad's running orders for that first section of the train designated it. A baggage car loaded with provisions for the picnic was hitched to the rear of the train—instead of being placed, as was customary, behind the tender—and locked to thwart hungry boys. The refreshments included ice and ice cream, both of which filled undreamed-of needs within two hours.

Conductor Alfred Hoppel, in command of the special, fretted to young Henry Harris, its twenty-one-year-old engineer, over the

A staff artist for Frank Leslie's Illustrated Newspaper went as soon as possible to the scene of the head-on train collision at Camp Hill, Pennsylvania, on July 17, 1856. He drew this somewhat exaggerated version of the "Appalling Disaster on the Northern Pennsylvania Railroad," as well as the other illustrations reproduced in this chapter, for the weekly's August 2nd issue.

fact that the stationmaster was obliging them to wait for more passengers when the train was already overloaded. They had been given an hour's time to get to Fort Washington. Ordinarily, that would be more than ample, but both men knew that their locomotive, *Shackamaxon*, would have trouble pulling a train as long and weighty as the one to which it was attached today.

After a delay of nearly ten minutes beyond the appointed departure time, Excursion No. 1 was finally allowed to leave. *Shackamaxon* hauled it through the waking city at a noticeably labored pace. Once the locomotive had struggled out into the shady countryside, it found the going even harder. Not only was it plagued by an insufficient head of steam; there was also a heavy dew on the iron rails, which sunlight had not yet reached. *Shackamaxon*'s driving wheels spun fruitlessly on the slippery track whenever they encountered an upgrade. At least twice the train was halted for several minutes before the engineer could "put enough dust on the rails," as one onlooker described the action, to enable the engine's wheels to take hold and move the cars forward.

"If this keeps up," Conductor Hoppel remarked irritatedly to his assistant after the second stall, "we'll have to take the siding at Edge Hill."

"Better keep to the main track and let the local take the siding," the assistant replied. "There are some dump cars on that siding. Not enough room for us."

Hoppel made no comment, but he was worried.

Regular trains on the NPRR, as on other lines of that day, were run according to printed instructions and the timetable. The instructions were posted in each locomotive cab. They were also memorized by conductors, whose responsibility it was to keep train movements in step with the timetable as closely as possible and yet maintain safety.

Whenever a special train was scheduled, its engineer and conductor were given handwritten instructions governing its movement, so that it would not interfere with normal traffic.

Hoppel's written orders for running Excursion No. 1 assured him that he had a clear track all the way to Fort Washington if he got there by 6 A.M. It was assumed that this would be easy to do. His train, after unloading its cargo of picnickers, was then to "follow the flag" of the Gwynedd local back to Philadelphia. *But if for any reason the excursion train should fall more than fifteen minutes behind schedule,* it was to take to a siding and "be kept out of way of regular trains."

In his uneasy thoughts, Hoppel weighed this last instruction against the familiar printed rule that ordered a conductor of a regularly scheduled train to wait fifteen minutes at any station where an expected arrival from the opposite direction had failed to appear on time.

Hoppel knew the local's schedule intimately, for that was his usual run. The local regularly left Gwynedd at 6 A.M., and Fort Washington at 6:15. If Excursion No. 1 was prevented from reaching Fort Washington before the local got there, would the conductor of the local wait fifteen minutes, as he was supposed to do?

The answer to this question was of crucial importance, because the siding at Edge Hill, three stops nearer Philadelphia, was the only place within several miles of Fort Washington where one of the trains could turn aside to let the other pass.

Hoppel's replacement as conductor of the local this morning was twenty-nine-year-old William Vanstavoren, a former molder and brakeman, not as experienced as Hoppel at being in command of a train, but a widely respected young man. Could he be expected to follow the rules? Hoppel thought he could.

On some American railroads at this time, telegraph systems were already in use to help keep track of the whereabouts of trains, but not on the North Pennsylvania. Its conductors and engineers were obliged to put their trust in their instructions, the timetables, their watches, and their eyesight. They couldn't be sure of the location of any train they couldn't see.

Tired *Shackamaxon* by now had climbed its last upgrade, and was settling comfortably into an accelerating run downhill, a fairly substantial incline that continued past Edge Hill, York Road, and Camp Hill, almost to Fort Washington. Excursion No. 1 began making brisk progress. Hoppel sent word back to the brakemen to take up the slack in the brake chains on each car, so that the brakes would respond faster when needed.

By the time the special reached Edge Hill, Hoppel's watch read 6:15. His train was already fifteen minutes behind schedule. He should have ordered it onto the siding. Instead, without consulting anyone, he decided to take a chance that Vanstavoren was holding the local at Fort Washington until the excursion train arrived. Hoppel ordered his engineer to stay on the main track and keep moving as fast as he could. The conductor was ordinarily a prudent and cautious man; many persons testified to that at his subsequent trial. But this was a fatally rash decision.

The Gwynedd local, according to eventual testimony, had begun its run precisely at 6:00 that morning. Among its score of passengers was a well-known Philadelphia newspaper reporter, Stephen A. Winslow. It was largely due to his presence that press coverage of the spectacular collision that followed was prompt, detailed, and accurate. Railroads then, and for many years afterward, ordinarily not only failed to release information about their wrecks, they did everything they could to prevent reporters from obtaining it. Reporter Winslow saw and heard this particular news happen.

At Fort Washington, where the local pulled in at 6:12, Winslow heard Vanstavoren call out to a boarding passenger, "Hasn't the special arrived yet?" When the passenger said No, the conductor remarked, "It should be up by now."

Winslow himself then asked Vanstavoren if he didn't intend to wait for the special.

"I'm not waiting for anybody," said the conductor.

After the accident, he said he had assumed that since the special was already fifteen minutes late, it must be waiting for him at Edge Hill. It would have been ridiculous, he said, for each train to be waiting vainly for the other.

Winslow and a companion were so alarmed at the prospect of danger that they did not return to their seats, but chose instead to ride on the rear platform of the single passenger car, at the end of the three-car train.

Their concern was shared by Engineer Lee, who asked Vanstavoren, "What did your orders say about it?"

"I have no orders," Vanstavoren replied.

"What are you going to do?"

"Go on," said the conductor.

"Very well," Lee answered, "but I think you'd better not."

"It's all right," said Vanstavoren. "Just sound your whistle like hell and go slow."

Lee was "fearful," he later confessed, but the conductor was in command. Lee didn't wish to be reported for disobeying orders. He eased *Aramingo* and her short train out of Fort Wash-

As soon as the dead could be snatched from the burning cars, they were laid out in a blacksmith's shop close by and there identified, in so far as that was possible. The maudlin press of the day made much of the fact that a woman boarder from a summer hotel not far from Camp Hill rescued and nursed an abandoned and presumably motherless baby she found squalling in the wreckage of the excursion train.

ington and proceeded toward Philadelphia at about 10 miles an hour, tooting his whistle repeatedly.

Excursion No. 1, meanwhile, was rattling down the long grade toward Camp Hill and across the resounding trestle south of the settlement at 35 mph. The customary blue flags that warned engineers to be cautious crossing the trestle were standing beside the track as usual, but caution had been abandoned. Thirty-five miles an hour was perilously fast for a heavy train with no means of stopping but a reversed engine and inefficient, slow-acting hand brakes, and with a blind curve at the bottom of the grade.

The line of the NPRR through the tiny settlement of Camp Hill—a cluster of two boardinghouses, a private residence, a blacksmith shop, and a shed—ran straight for nearly five hundred yards, mostly along the top of a 26-foot embankment. There were curves at both ends of the straight stretch, and they faced in opposite directions. Both cut through high banks, which reduced forward visibility within the curves to a few feet. On a map, this portion of the route would have looked like a very elongated S, drawn backward. The local had rounded the top curve and crossed most of the straight section of track before the excursion train swung around the bottom curve and found the loitering local directly in its path.

Lee and the train crew of the local did everything possible to avoid a crash, but Excursion No. 1 was coming much too fast to stop in a hundred yards. Even in his desperate haste, Lee noted with surprise that he had heard no whistle from the special. (That was doubtless because he had been making so much noise with his own.) What surprised him even more, he recalled afterward, was that he couldn't see anyone aboard the oncoming engine. That was because *Shackamaxon*'s youthful driver had jumped as soon as he had reversed his engine. The fireman had followed suit. Engineer Harris fell between locomotive and tender and was killed. The fireman was at first reported missing, but was soon found, "awfully cut and bruised."

A few moments before the crash, Thomas Harkins, a member of the parish committee in charge of the picnic, had been strolling through the excursion cars, making sure that his charges were in a holiday mood. "Everyone seemed satisfied," he reported. In the first car, he had noticed Father Daniel Sheridan, pastor of St. Michael's, chatting with one of his fellow committeemen just inside the open forward door of the car. Beyond them, the tender bobbed and dodged. That was the last time Harkins saw Father Sheridan alive. When next he gazed at him, a dreadful quarter-hour later, the priest was a corpse, his body caught between the wrecked locomotive and the car in which he had been riding. The fire hadn't reached him.

Harkins's own life had been saved because he had moved back to the third or fourth car by the time the collision occurred. Without the slightest warning, he had there been hurled against one wall of the car, and in his painful shock and confusion had thought the train had been hit from behind. When he was able to crawl out of the wreckage, the fourth car was beginning to smolder. Harkins's hair and eyebrows were singed before he could roll down the embankment. He landed up against a pair of car wheels that had been torn off in the crash. Making sure that he wasn't injured, he scrambled up the slope toward the ruined excursion train, whose first five cars were by now ablaze. It was then that he discovered Father Sheridan's body, though he could do nothing to rescue it because the heat of the flames was so intense.

A few minutes earlier, Brakeman Lewis Pease had reached the open platform between the second and third cars on his assigned task of taking up the slack in the brakes. "We were going at a pretty good gait," he later declared. Pease found a young man standing on the platform, and warned him that it was a dangerous thing to do, and contrary to the rules.

He had barely finished talking when he heard the whistled signal "Down brakes!", though he couldn't tell whether it came from the engine of his own train or from another. Almost simultaneously, Conductor Hoppel emerged from the rear door of the second car and the trains collided.

Hoppel and Pease were hurled down the embankment, Hoppel breaking a leg as he landed. The young man who had been standing on the platform was crushed to death.

When Hoppel, temporarily knocked out, regained consciousness, the first object he saw was a pink dress lying in the grass. It was not quite the color of danger, but it would do for a warning signal. With a true railroader's instinct, he promptly ripped the dress in half and, by messengers from the ranks of would-be rescuers, "sent a piece both ways along the road to warn approaching trains."

Hoppel's excitement and agitation made him scarcely aware of his injury for a few moments. He then collapsed. One of the men who helped carry him on an improvised stretcher to Fort Washington heard him exclaim, "My God, why didn't Bill wait his fifteen minutes!"

The sound of the crash had been heard as far as Fort Washington, a mile away, as well as in Camp Hill and throughout the surrounding farm community. Smoke from the burning cars was visible for miles. Summer boarders and local farmers hurried to the scene as fast as their horses or their legs could carry them, and immediately devised ways to help the victims.

"The groans and shouts of the wounded and those held by the legs or arms to the burning wreck," a survivor of the crash reported, "were of a character to appall the bravest heart."

Men prevented from dragging injured or dead persons out of the debris because of the blistering heat of the fire quickly formed a bucket line, leading up from a small brook. Their strenuous efforts to douse the flames were unsuccessful, though, until reinforced by those of the Chestnut Hill Fire Company, which soon arrived with its hose cart. With joined forces, the firemen were able not only to prevent the remaining five cars of the train from being consumed in the blaze but before long had dampened the fire enough to make possible the removal of the dead.

Women of the neighborhood spread out through the adjacent meadow, now littered with the injured who had been carried there. The day was rapidly developing into a scorcher, early though it was, and some of the volunteer nurses were soon distributing ice and ice cream, which someone had remembered and had retrieved by breaking into the locked baggage car.

William Swain, of Chestnut Hill, who arrived at about this time, declared that "the scene was the most awful I ever witnessed. Of five cars, nothing was left standing but the wheels. Every bit of woodwork was totally destroyed."

The blacksmith shop and shed in Camp Hill had been converted into temporary morgues. The solitary residence there had been offered by its owner for use as a dressing station for the injured. Doctors summoned from all the nearest towns began galloping up in their buggies. Not long afterward, a carload of Philadelphia doctors and nurses arrived, with abundant medical supplies. Among the city physicians was young S. Weir Mitchell, the future famed neurologist and romantic novelist, then twenty-seven years old. This large medical rescue team had been hastily assembled and dispatched by railroad officials, notified of the disaster by police telegraph.

Excursion No. 1 had sustained almost all of the damage of the head-on collision. The local's locomotive, *Aramingo*, had been smashed and overthrown, and its baggage car was split open, but there had been no fire on that side of the crash. Most of the twenty-odd persons aboard had escaped serious injury and extricated themselves without difficulty. The principal exception was Joseph Edwards, the train's baggagemaster, whose legs were broken.

When the local's engineer, William Lee, "fearful that my engine would fly from the track," had jumped and tumbled down into the meadow an instant before the collision, he shortly found Edwards there, pale and helpless, in the long grass. Lee also encountered his conductor, Vanstavoren, in a state of hysterical despair over the wreck, for which he held himself solely to blame. Vanstavoren retained sufficient presence of mind to ask Lee to help Edwards, and then made dazed and ineffective efforts himself to care for some of the other injured. He and Lee soon started for Edge Hill, as fast as they could walk or run, to take the news to Philadelphia and spur help to the scene of the accident. At Edge Hill they found a handcar, and pumped it down the tracks for a mile. At Tacony, they finally caught a horse-drawn stage into the city. On the way, Vanstavoren, whom Lee had been trying to console, said passionately, "If I had a dose of arsenic, I'd take it."

They parted in Philadelphia about nine o'clock. A few minutes later, Vanstavoren did indeed procure and swallow an ounce of arsenic, following it with three ounces of morphine. He then went to the railroad office and asked if he should turn himself in to the police. Even as he spoke he came violently sick, and was taken home. A doctor was called in at 1 P.M., but by then there was nothing he could do to stop the progress of the poison. A few minutes before five o'clock, Vanstavoren died.

By two o'clock that afternoon, the movable injured had been treated in the meadow at Camp Hill or in Fort Washington, the identifiable dead collected, and a train made up of surviving cars from Excursion No. 1 carried them all back to Philadelphia at a funereal pace. News of the catastrophe had already spread through the city with nearly the speed of telegraphy. As the train rolled slowly between rows of tenements and frame houses, hundreds of people hung out of their windows to watch in silent sympathy.

A frantic mob of around two thousand relatives and friends of the picnickers, only partially restrained by an augmented police force, swarmed to greet the train as it pulled into the outermost city station. Many of these same people had earlier fought unsuccessfully with railroadmen to let them ride handcars to the scene of the accident. Some had managed at last to climb aboard a train of baggage cars headed in that direction, a few of them even riding the locomotive's cowcatcher. When they got to Camp Hill, "their shrieks had mingled with those of the dying." The majority had had to remain behind, their anxiety rising as they waited without news of who had been saved and who had not. Now, at last, the tangible evidence was before their eyes. The final count was sixty killed and sixty injured—"maimed and crippled, perhaps for life," a district attorney said.

That night, William Lee, engineer of the local, was arrested and taken to the Fourth Street jail. This was only a formality, until a coroner's inquest could be held. Nobody seriously thought Lee had caused the accident, but he was the only engineer involved who was still available. The sole surviving conductor, Hoppel, of Excursion No. 1, still lay at Fort Washington.

A coroner's jury on July 25th held Hoppel responsible for the calamity, his guilt being implicit in his running orders, which had directed him to place his train on a siding if it were more than fifteen minutes late. It was twenty-three minutes late at the time of the collision.

The jury, absolving both Vanstavoren and Lee of blame for the wreck, found that "the immediate cause of the collision was the gross carelessness of Alfred F. Hoppel. . . . We find that if the regulations of the Railroad Company had been obeyed, the collision would not have happened."

This last statement was ambiguous. Vanstavoren, too, had disobeyed regulations, though with slightly better justification.

Hoppel was arrested at once and sent to prison at Norristown, county seat of Montgomery County, in which the accident had occurred. He was to await trial for "murder." A month later, a grand jury at Norristown indicted him on a charge of manslaughter. His trial was postponed until November, and he was released on $10,000 bond.

At the trial, which began November 14th and ended five days later, skillful defense lawyers were able to persuade the jury that blame for the Camp Hill disaster was at least as much Vanstavoren's as Hoppel's—a point of view seemingly confirmed by Vanstavoren's suicide—and that justice would not be served by punishing the only survivor. After arguing the matter for several hours, the jury finally agreed with the defense. At 10:15 P.M. on November 19th, it found Hoppel "not guilty."

4

Incident at Big Sisters Creek
(Angola, New York: December 18, 1867)

THE railroad wreck that occurred near the little station at
Angola, New York, some twenty-one miles west of Buffalo,
on the bleak afternoon of December 18, 1867, has been known
ever since as the Angola Horror. That was the name conferred
upon it by many a newspaper headline-writer within the week
that followed, and the name has persisted in history.

What seared the memory of this accident into the public mind
was not its novelty, for wooden cars heated by wood- or coal-
burning stoves invariably caught fire when smashed, and some
passengers usually died in the flames. Nor was it the pathetic
fact that the disaster took place in the merriest season of the
year, a week before Christmas. The death toll in several previous
railway wrecks had been substantially higher. Moreover, at Angola, only two cars were derailed and demolished. In one of
them, though forty passengers were hurt, only a single life was
lost, and not by fire. In the other car, however, the last one on
the eastbound *New York Express* of the Lake Shore Railroad,
destruction was nearly total. Here, indeed, was true horror. Of
forty-four passengers in that last car, which was consumed to its
blackened ironwork, only three escaped, and they were injured.

The *New York Express* was running two hours and twenty-five
minutes late, but not hurrying, when it passed through Angola
at 3:10 P.M., on December 18th. Earlier in the day, a freight
train had been derailed on the line, east of Erie, Pennsylvania,
and the Lake Shore Railroad's assistant superintendent in charge
of operations had telegraphed the conductor of the express to let
his passengers have lunch at Erie. They were going to have to
wait quite a while before the track ahead was cleared, and they
might as well pass the time and bolster their spirits by eating.

When the *New York Express* was finally ordered to proceed
eastward from Erie, its engineer, Charles Carscadin, made no

effort to make up lost time, but kept the train rolling at its normal average speed of about 30 mph. There was no pressing need to hurry, for the only connection to be concerned about was scheduled for six o'clock that evening at Buffalo. Even after the long delay at Erie, Carscadin expected to bring his train into Buffalo with at least two hours to spare.

The engineer was a veteran of fifteen years' service on the road, and known to be a sober and cautious man. The train he was driving this winter afternoon along the ice-slick eastern shore of Lake Erie consisted of three baggage cars, a second-class passenger car, and three first-class passenger cars, the last two of which belonged to other railroads. The second coach from the rear came from the Cleveland & Erie, which had track of the same gauge as the Lake Shore's: 4 feet 10 inches. The last car of the train belonged to the Cleveland & Toledo, which had a track gauge of 4 feet 9¼ inches.

There were scores of small railroads in the United States at the time, and seldom did their gauges match; they ranged from 4 feet 8½ inches to 7 feet. A definite trend was under way to establish the lower extreme as the national standard, thus eliminating a great deal of bother for connecting railroads and much inconvenience for long-distance travelers. The trend had been given a powerful boost in 1862, when Congress set 4 feet 8½ inches as the gauge for the Union Pacific and Central Pacific railroads, soon to begin laying track in each other's direction from Omaha and Sacramento. The trend was by no means widespread yet, however; nearly half the nation's track mileage still consisted of gauges other than 4 feet 8½ inches. As a result of this awkward lack of standardization, some connecting lines had adopted the dangerous practice of using so-called "compromise" cars, with wheels that had extra-wide flanges, enabling them— or so it was intended—to run on tracks varying in gauge by as much as one inch or even an inch and a half.

The better-managed railroads refused to use compromise cars, because of the hazard involved. Unfortunately, the Cleveland & Toledo was not one of these. Its coach No. 21, which rode on December 18th at the tail end of the *New York Express,* was a compromise car. Furthermore, it had an undetected defect that increased the riskiness of running it on track three-quarters of an inch wider than the track for which it was primarily intended: The forward axle of its rear truck was bent upward, giving the

An artist's conception of the moment when the last car of the eastbound New York Express, having been dragged in a derailed state nearly across the bridge over Big Sisters Creek at Angola, New York, on December 18, 1867, broke away from the train and fell 40 feet into the icy ravine below. The second coach from the rear is shown about to roll off the track in the opposite direction.

wheels attached to it a slightly bowlegged stance and narrowing their tread a tiny fraction of an inch more than usual. This defect was not perceptible to the eye when the car was standing still, so no wheel inspector had been inspired to measure the distance between the wheel flanges at several points and discover that they were not quite parallel.

This defect might have escaped notice forever if the right-hand wheel on that axle had not slipped off the rail at a newly installed frog leading onto a siding a few hundred feet east of the Angola station. In dropping onto the ties, the wayward wheel threw the rear end of the last car off the rails to the left just as the engine began crossing a long open-deck bridge 50 feet above the steep, frozen banks of Big Sisters Creek.

At the point west of Angola where it was customary for locals to start slowing for a stop at the station, Engineer Carscadin had cut off steam and begun coasting the *New York Express* at 25–30 mph down the slight grade that continued through the village and across Big Sisters Bridge. Expresses never stopped at Angola except on special orders, but firemen on eastbound expresses routinely oiled the engine valves there, and engineers had to shut off steam while their firemen moved out cautiously along the engine running boards, clinging to the handrails, and performed this essential chore.

The tip of the locomotive's pilot had already passed the trackside warning sign that read "Slow" and was nearly at the bridge when the emergency bell in Carscadin's cab sharply clanged. The engineer immediately tooted "Down brakes." There were only two brakemen on the entire train, however, and their response, however prompt, could not produce instant results. The locomotive rolled on across the bridge.

Then the bell rang again. This time Carscadin opened the steam valve fully and reversed the engine. He then kneeled on his seat cushion and leaned far out the window, peering back to see what had gone wrong. He had felt a slight jerk in the forward motion of the train, but nothing more. Wind off the lake swirled smoke and steam around his head and shut off his view toward the rear as the wheels were sliding to a stop. The front end of the train came to rest 2,504 feet beyond the point where the last car was derailed. Not until the train had been halted, and the engineer had run back along the track to the rear platform, did he discover he had lost two cars. They lay in the ravine on opposite sides of the bridge. Smoke was already billowing up from the one to the north.

John Martin, who owned a tin-and-hardware store in Angola, had been on the freight-house platform loading supplies onto his wagon when the express went past the station. He had watched it for a moment or two longer, and thus became the sole eyewitness to the entire tragedy that ensued. When Martin saw the last car lurch to the left as it crossed the switching-point east of the station, he realized what had happened, and ran down the track after the train, swinging his hat and shouting to rouse the neighborhood. He saw the end car dragged sideways nearly the whole length of the bridge before its front coupling broke and the car plunged, hind end first, 40 feet down the ravine. "I then saw the second car scoot the other way," Martin afterward told a coroner's jury. "It rolled off sideways like a saw log."

Martin ran across the slippery bridge on the ties and was among the first rescuers to reach the fallen cars. Passengers piled out of the undamaged portion of the train, which had come to a stop just beyond the bridge, and residents of Angola ran from their houses and shops to help the injured. Their efforts in behalf of the victims trapped in the last car were almost entirely ineffectual, however. That car had landed upside down on its hind end, close to the bottom of the ravine, and lay at an angle of 45 degrees up the ice-covered slope. When it struck the ground, it collapsed, and passengers, seats, luggage, and portions of the flimsy framework were dumped at the rear end of the car, cascading on top of the stove there. At the same time, the stove at the front end of the car, torn from its inadequate moorings, showered embers upon the heaped tinder below. The floor of the crushed and overturned car rested barely three feet above its roof, and the space between them quickly became a roaring flue.

It was nearly impossible for would-be rescuers to reach that car. Those attempting to approach from above couldn't prevent themselves from sliding past it. Those trying to climb up to it from below could not get a dependable foothold on the crusted bank.

An especially eerie incident occurred as these desperate efforts were in progress. There was a sudden fusillade of shots from inside the blazing wreckage, and a bullet tore through one pant leg of a man standing on the track above. Evidently, a passenger in the car had been carrying a revolver on his person or in his

© HARPER'S WEEKLY, January 11, 1868

*Fire consumed the last car and all but three of its forty-four passengers
before men from the rest of the train and the nearby village could help
them escape. At first, the slopes were too slippery to enable rescuers to
reach the smashed and overturned car; soon the fire was too intense to
make rescues possible.*

luggage, and the heat had discharged it.

Two passengers had somehow managed to escape from the top
end of this car almost immediately after it crashed, for John Martin had seen them clawing their way up to the track when he ran
toward the wreck. A third passenger in the rear car was finally

The next-to-last car of the New York Express rolled off the track just beyond the bridge, and slid down a crusted slope to a far gentler landing than the last car had. All of its passengers but one were recovered alive, though forty were injured.

hauled out from the top of the wreckage by a human chain, its linked arms extended to him down the bank from the rear platform of the standing train. Then the intense heat drove the crowd back, and no more could be done for anyone aboard the car.

The second derailed coach, from which a few fortunate people had fled into the car ahead when it began thumping over the rails, had cleared the bridge before it "rolled sideways like a saw log." It had slid down a gentler slope and lay on one side, fairly intact. The framework caught fire, but a crowd of rescuers, one of them armed with five milk pails he had gathered on the run from a nearby farmhouse, quickly put out the flames by tossing scoops of snow on them. The footing was much firmer here, and all occupants of the car were taken out alive, except for a man who had been instantly killed when the derailed car slammed against a fallen tree.

The tragedy occurred on a Wednesday afternoon. On the following Sunday, a huge civic funeral was held in Buffalo for nineteen victims who could not be identified. With singular lack of concern for its public image, the Lake Shore Railroad staged the funeral in the Central Depot. There, at 2 P.M., eight thousand persons gathered to hear massed choirs from the city's churches sing "I Would Not Live Alway" and "Solemn Sounds the Funeral Note."

After appropriate ceremonies, wagons of the American Express Company, each draped in black and drawn by four bay horses, bore the coffins through central Buffalo, past ranks of onlookers, to St. Paul's Episcopal Church. The wagons were followed by carriages, in which rode the mayor, the city council, officials of the railroad, and other local notables. At St. Paul's, the burial service was held, for the coffins were all placed in a vault beneath the cathedral.

For all its grimness, the Angola Horror helped bring about three highly beneficial developments. It immediately put an end to the use of compromise cars. It hastened the standardization of track gauges. Most importantly, it lent special urgency to the inventive efforts of twenty-one-year-old George Westinghouse, in the New York village of Central Bridge, to devise a train brake that could be operated by compressed air from the engine. A year and a half after the wreck at Angola, Westinghouse succeeded in patenting his automatic air brake, probably the greatest single contribution ever made to railway safety. If the *New York Express* could have been equipped with Westinghouse brakes, the derailed cars would never have been dragged as far as the bridge, and the Angola Horror would not have happened.

5

For Want of a Bell-Rope
(New Hamburg, New York: February 6, 1871)

IT was nearly twelve years after former railroad conductor Edwin Drake had brought in the nation's first oil well before the ultimate danger inherent in transporting by rail this highly combustible liquid—"an explosive scarcely less terrible than gunpowder"—was demonstrated in a flaming wintry wreck beside the Hudson River that killed more than a score of persons.

"Extra No. 3," a Hudson River Railroad mixed freight of twenty-five cars, was lumbering down the east bank of the river in midevening of February 6, 1871, a Monday night of deep cold and bright moonlight. There were fifteen oil cars in the train's consist, some of them roofed and slatted and containing refined oil in barrels. Seven of them were tankers, loaded with crude oil, which rode at approximately the center of the string of cars.

As the slow freight emerged downgrade from a tunnel north of the station at New Hamburg, a village about fifty-six miles above New York City, a flagman standing near the tunnel mouth noticed that one of the tankers was thumping over the rails. An axle had broken. The flagman waved his lantern and shouted in the engineer's direction, but Engineer Cornelius Row neither saw nor heard him. A few men in or near the station did, however. They ran out toward the passing freight, yelling "Stop!"

Their cries roused the train's conductor, Edgar Underwood, who was warming himself beside the stove in the caboose, along with two of the freight's required three brakemen. One of the latter should have been at his assigned post in midtrain, where he could signal both engineer and conductor with his lantern if the need arose. Instead, with the conductor's tacit consent, he was enjoying the relative comforts of the caboose. The night, after all, was frigid, and Underwood, as will shortly be seen, was most casual about observing rules and regulations. The third brakeman was up front in the locomotive, where he was supposed to be.

Spurred into sudden action by the shouts outside the caboose, Conductor Underwood sent one brakeman scampering to the roof to start twisting the wheel of the hand brake. He told the other to hop off the train, then rumbling along at only 8 to 10 mph, and tell the telegraph operator at New Hamburg to tap out word that the Extra No. 3 freight had broken down. Meanwhile, grabbing his lantern, he hurried onto the rear platform, leaned far out facing forward, and several times in quick succession let his lantern appear to drop from his outstretched hand. That was the regulation light signal to the engineer to stop the train. This time, though, no one in the locomotive was looking his way. The train ambled on toward the 200-foot low trestle across Wappinger's Creek, a quarter-mile south of the New Hamburg station.

In the middle of the trestle was a drawbridge, which often had to be opened in summer but in winter was invariably closed, for the creek froze nearly solid. The ice lay thick upon the water on this February night; in fact, two or three small schooners near the north end of the trestle were frozen fast at their moorings. Above the drawbridge, which accommodated two tracks, hung a signal light at the top of a pole. The bridge-tender had to climb a thirty-four-foot ladder to change the light from white, which signified that the bridge was closed and trains could safely proceed, to red, which warned that the draw was open. This tedious task was a frequent chore on summer evenings; in winter, however, because the bridge was never opened, the light shone white up and down the tracks every night. The bridge-tender's sole concern was to make sure that it didn't go out. It was lighted this particular evening; he had just seen to that before the freight appeared.

For a couple of minutes after Conductor Underwood began his urgent signaling with the lantern, the engineer of the freight made no apparent effort to stop. During those long two minutes, Underwood had reason to regret sharply that he had disobeyed a new company rule at the beginning of the trip.

During the previous November, Superintendent J. M. Toucey of the Hudson River Railroad had issued an order that henceforth all freight trains must carry and use signal-bell ropes, extending from caboose to locomotive cab. These were already

This lurid conception of the instant of collision between the Hudson River Railroad's upbound Pacific Express *and the derailed oil tanker of a downbound freight on the night of February 6, 1871, is inaccurate in some details but realistically depicts the explosiveness of the fire that was immediately ignited. The picture was drawn for* Frank Leslie's Illustrated Newspaper.

standard equipment on HRRR passenger trains but had been used only occasionally on freights. Toucey intended to remedy that dangerous deficiency, but compliance with his order was neither eager nor prompt. Underwood, for one, didn't favor bell-ropes on freights. He said they were a nuisance; that they were ordinarily threaded through the brake wheels on the roofs of boxcars, where they sometimes got snarled; that there was really no place to put them on tank cars; and anyway, he added, it took the combined strength of two men in the caboose to pull the rope hard enough to ring the bell in the engine cab.

About all a bell-rope on a freight was good for, Underwood declared, was to warn the engineer by its violent yank at the bell in case the train broke apart. That was precisely what was about to happen at New Hamburg. Unfortunately, the regulation bell-rope lay coiled in the caboose. Underwood had decided it wasn't necessary on this trip.

The crippled tank car somehow held to the down track until it reached the drawbridge. There, the dragging end of the broken axle dropped between ties, and the car did a half-somersault, severing its connection with the forward part of the train and flopping sideways across the parallel track. By now, Engineer Row was well aware of what had happened, and braked his train to a stop. The first fifteen cars had cleared the trestle.

Instantly, what was uppermost in the minds of the train crew and of those men running to the scene from New Hamburg was the terrifying thought that the railroad's *Pacific Express,* up-bound for Albany and points west, would be along any minute on the track now blocked by the derailed tanker. It was, in fact, already overdue; the two trains should have passed each other five miles north of New Hamburg.

As the startled bridge-tender hurried toward him, Engineer Row, jumping down from his cab, yelled, "For God's sake, get out your red light!" Without waiting to see that the other man complied, Row, clutching his own red lantern, started running south between the tracks. His fireman and the front brakeman, also carrying lanterns, followed close behind.

For a second or two, the bridge-tender considered climbing the ladder to the top of the pole on the drawbridge and exchanging the white light for a red one, but decided that would take too long. Instead, he snatched up the danger signal and ran down the track after the other men.

The headlight of the *Pacific Express* had already flashed into view, two miles south. The train, drawn by a locomotive named *Constitution,* had left New York City five minutes behind its scheduled 8:00 P.M. departure time and was now running seventeen minutes late. It was made up of a baggage car, a mail-and-express car, five sleepers, and a coach at the tail end. Just before the express had pulled out of Manhattan's Thirtieth Street station, Superintendent Toucey had cautioned its engineer, "Doc"

Another view of the fiery wreck at New Hamburg, New York, drawn for Frank Leslie's Illustrated Newspaper, shows the scene as the artist, guided by news accounts, imagined it looked just after the locomotive, baggage car, and mail car had sunk into Wappinger's Creek and a spreading sea of flaming oil was surrounding the first three sleeping cars and ten freight cars, the latter hidden from view.

Simmons, not to exceed normal speeds in case he started losing time, for it was a bitter night, the kind of weather that made iron axles even more brittle than usual. With this warning in mind, Simmons was driving the *Pacific Express* at about 30 mph when it rounded a bend near the water tank at Old Troy and he and his fireman first noted the familiar white light above the drawbridge at New Hamburg. They were only a half-mile away from it when they noticed that between them and the drawbridge several red lights were bobbing and swaying close to the track.

"I guess something's the matter with the draw," exclaimed the fireman, Nicholas Tallon.

Promptly, the engineer three times in succession sounded the two quick toots of the whistle that signaled his brakemen to apply the hand brakes. Then he called out to Tallon, "Put on the patents!" This was the railroadman's expression for a new braking system. Subsequent newspaper reports and court testimony never made quite clear how these "patent brakes" functioned, though it was apparent that they were spring-actuated, and that the springs were released by cords strung through the cars to the locomotive cab. Either the engineer or the fireman could pull the cords if he needed to stop the train in a hurry. The only trouble was, as the fireman later explained, the slack in the line was such that one had to haul in about eighteen feet of cord before the strong springs slapped the brakes on.

Tallon had no more than begun this burdensome process when, realizing how close they were getting to the drawbridge, he said, "We'd better jump." Engineer Simmons, he recalled, "simply looked at me and turned away." Tallon jumped.

Simmons, at full throttle, reversed the driving wheels of the *Constitution*. Skaters on Wappinger's Creek saw the locomotive puff furiously and sparks fly from its back-spinning drivers. This last-minute effort retarded the train only slightly, for not only had Tallon abandoned the "patents," but the brakemen, as they explained later, hadn't had time to apply the hand brakes before the crash came.

Constitution plowed into the fallen tank car, ripping it open and drenching engine cab and tender with a shower of crude oil. The instant the oil came in contact with the locomotive's firebox, it ignited explosively, and billowing flames swept across the full spread of thick black liquid that was flowing over the ice, like syrup leaking from a broken pitcher. The locomotive at once

On the second day after the wreck, salvagers are shown recovering bodies and possessions from the icy waters of Wappinger's Creek while, at the same time, railroad workmen are beginning to rebuild the burned drawbridge and trestle. The Hudson River is at right in this drawing from Frank Leslie's Illustrated Newspaper.

toppled into Wappinger's Creek, plunging through the ice and dragging tender, baggage car, and mail car into the water after it. The first sleeping car, its doors locked from the outside—as was customary, to thwart thieves—was slung against the blazing tank car and caught fire from end to end. The flames quickly enveloped the nine stranded freight cars on the adjoining track. These soon poured additional oil on the blaze, and the fire boiled upward to a height of a hundred and fifty feet, flickeringly illuminating the snowy hills and ice-covered Hudson for miles.

The time of collision was precisely determined: When they fished the body of Engineer Simmons out from under the ice next day, his watch was found to have stopped at 10:25 P.M.

One of the passengers in the coach at the rear of the *Pacific Express* was General R. W. Judson, an attorney from Ogdensburg, New York. He told of jumping off the train after the "concussion" to see what had happened, and of running forward, to find "the first sleeping car a sheet of fire, not a sound coming from it except the crackling of the flames. The passengers on the other cars scrambled out as soon as they could, the flames, like lightning, communicating to the rest of the train, and two more sleeping cars were destroyed. The passengers and railroad employees uncoupled the balance of the train, consisting of two more sleeping cars and an ordinary passenger car, and pushed them down the track.

"The bridge caught fire and burned rapidly," General Judson continued, "there being no means at hand to extinguish the flames. News being sent to a town nearby, a steam fire-engine was sent down in less than an hour, and was instrumental in saving several schooners lying near the bridge, which caught fire. The bridge was burned before the arrival of the engine."

Rescue efforts by New Hamburg residents were prompt and solicitous, though somewhat marred by the behavior of two drunks, whose unseemly actions and leering remarks attracted the attention of a reporter and received greatly exaggerated coverage in a New York City paper two days later. This reporter likened the citizens of New Hamburg to those coastal residents of former times who used to entice vessels onto rocks with false beacons in order to wreck the ships and plunder them and their passengers. This libelous slur elicited an indignant letter to the editor from a group of New Hamburgians, who wrote, in part: "One report said that half of the houses of this village were furnished from the wreck. The smart individual who wrote that report certainly must have had a very correct idea of the amount of furniture that could be taken from one sleeping-coach with one-half burned to a coal and the other half buried six feet under water. There can be no doubt but he has a chimerical imagination."

Work on a new bridge and salvage operations to retrieve what was left of the express, especially its sunken locomotive, began the day after the wreck. An onlooker noted that "the *Constitution*'s brasswork shimmers in the water, and her black, bruised smokestack is visible at low tide."

At the same time, a coroner's jury was convened, and its members soon heard Superintendent Toucey's catalogue of the various sins of commission and omission that had led to the collision. He said that there were printed orders that bell-ropes should be in use on all HRRR freights, that they should not be run through brake handles; and that only one brakeman at a time was to be allowed to warm himself in the caboose. Furthermore, Toucey declared, if all three brakemen had been on the job, the slow freight could have been stopped within two or three hundred feet, not a half-mile, as had happened. Toucey also stated that the bridge-tender might more usefully have changed the drawbridge signal to red than have run down the track waving his lantern.

As for the handling of the express train, Toucey declared that Engineer Simmons was at fault, and, in fact, in violation of orders, in not having told the fireman to apply the "patent brakes" before blowing the whistle, rather than afterward; that the "patents" had never failed to work when the cords were pulled properly; and that Fireman Tallon had obviously been far more concerned with his own safety than with applying the brakes. He added that the brakemen on the express had really had time enough to put on the hand brakes, even though they said they hadn't. However, Toucey went on, the jurors should appreciate the fact that, even with all braking appliances in effective use, the express couldn't have been halted in less than 1,500 feet. Conductor Charles Cossum of the express subsequently commented that a train of sleeping cars, weighing "thirty to forty tons," was harder to stop than a train of ordinary cars, weighing "eight to nine tons."

Members of the coroner's jury, meanwhile, had gone to view

the bodies of the twenty-two identified victims of the wreck, "then and there lying dead," including one young man whose father, ironically, had been lost in the Angola Horror a little more than three years earlier. The jurors had heard testimony from Toucey, members of both train crews, the bridge-tender, and several passengers on the express. After judicious consideration, they then placed all blame for the disaster at New Hamburg on the fact that, "from some reason to the jury unknown, the patent brakes were not effectively applied."

A joint investigating committee of the New York legislature had far more difficulty deciding what or who was at fault, and finally gave up trying. It held hearings at Albany in February and March. On March 7th, a Mr. Creamer of LaSalle, Illinois, whose first name was not disclosed but who was identified as the inventor of the parlous "patent brakes," was heard from *in absentia*. In a letter read aloud to the committee members, Creamer testily pointed out that it was the engineer, not the fireman, who was supposed to pull the brake cords—"till taut." Furthermore, wrote Creamer, his brakes had been in use for thirteen years and "never before had it ever been said that they failed." If applied properly, he declared, they could stop a train within eight or nine hundred feet.

The committee members, little aided in their probe by the inventor's querulous comments, confessed on April 14th that they were unable to agree upon a unanimous verdict, or even upon a majority opinion. Therefore, presenting three hundred pages of printed testimony to the legislature, they urged the members of that body to "come to a conclusion that shall suit themselves." No evidence can be found that the legislature ever gave the matter another thought.

Mr. Creamer's brakes were doubtless far inferior to Mr. Westinghouse's air brakes, which in 1871 were just beginning to gain acceptance, but it took an editorial writer for the New York *Times* to make the most perceptive observation on the basic reason for the fiery disaster at New Hamburg: "The want of a bell-rope on the oil train certainly facilitated, if it did not actually cause, the fatal collision."

6

A Sudden Blow from Behind
(Revere, Massachusetts: August 26, 1871)

EARLY on the misty Saturday evening of August 26, 1871, an impatient crowd thronged the Boston terminal of the Eastern Railroad, which ran trains between that city and Portland, Maine. The line served several suburban communities northeast of Boston, and many of the persons gathered in Causeway Street station that evening were bound for a camp meeting at Hamilton, twenty-one miles up the North Shore. A religious revival there had been attracting large numbers of both the devout and the curious for the previous ten days. Every night, all northbound trains had been late starting. These included, especially, locals that turned off the double-track main line onto the single-track Saugus branch line at Everett, three miles outside the city, and the Beverly locals, which took the main line all the way to their destination and became the revivalists' commuter-trains.

One reason for the epidemic of delayed departures was that the railroad, as an irate citizen complained in print, was "trying to do too much business with too few cars." A shortage of rolling stock was not the most serious of the Eastern Railroad's shortcomings, however. The road was not only shabbily equipped, it was shoddily run, and years behind the times. Its backwardness and inefficiency would be responsible, on this humid night, for one of the best-remembered wrecks of the 19th Century.

Four Eastern Railroad trains were scheduled to leave Causeway Street station each evening between 6:30 and 8:00. The first two were Saugus locals, the third a Beverly local, and the fourth, the *Bangor Express,* due to depart at 8:00. On August 26th the crowds were bigger and the locals later than ever. In the resulting confusion, the Beverly train went out between the two Saugus trains instead of behind the second, as it usually did.

The Beverly local was scheduled to depart at 7:15 P.M., and on this evening Charles T. Story, his wife, and small daughter were among those assembling to board it. The Storys were not headed for the camp meeting; they were going to visit friends in Beverly. The four-car local did not even enter the Boston station until it was time for it to leave, and in the rush for seats in its three coaches the Storys lost the chance to sit together. The father, holding his child in his lap, sat beside a male stranger in the first coach, just behind the baggage car; his wife sat in back of him, next to a highly nervous woman who soon became convinced that something awful was going to happen.

For thirty minutes the local continued to take on passengers, until all seats were taken, the aisles filled with standees, and the passengers in a thoroughly bad temper. At 7:45 it departed, three-quarters of an hour behind the first Saugus local, thirteen minutes ahead of the second Saugus local.

Meanwhile, the eight-o'clock *Bangor Express,* which would take the same track northeastward as the three other trains, was loading in the station. It had an oddly arranged consist: behind the engine *Newburyport* and its tender ranged—in a reversal of normal sequence—a smoker, a Pullman sleeper, a coach, and a baggage car. The express's engineer, Ashbel S. Brown, as a Boston reporter subsequently described him, was a fine-looking, intelligent man of about forty, well built, small of stature, and possessed of "a bright clear eye." But no one had told him, said Brown later, about the Beverly local's belated departure. He assumed that, according to the timetable, it was long since out of his way.

Just as Brown opened the throttle to move the express out of the station at 8:05, only five minutes late, the stationmaster came running up alongside the engine and called up to him, "Look out for the Saugus-branch train!" Brown said, "All right," and the express gathered speed. It was not long before the engineer caught sight of the rear lights of the second Saugus local. He was obliged to loiter behind them as far as Everett.

This railway game of tag caused much apprehension among the Beverly local's passengers. At Somerville, the first stop, there was a fanfare of locomotive whistling, fore and aft, that so disturbed passengers riding in the coach with the Story family that several of them shoved windows open and peered out into the mist and fog to see if they could find out the cause of the commotion. The conductor, who had begun collecting tickets, said loudly, "Please keep your seats. There's no danger."

With only a moderate degree of exaggeration, an artist for Frank Leslie's Illustrated Newspaper envisions the scene at Revere Station a few moments after the engine of the Bangor Express (right) telescoped the rear car of the Beverly local. Men are already hauling the remains of the shattered car off the top of the engine, and fire is spreading to the rest of the local.

As the local left Somerville, the man beside Charles Story leaned far out of his open window for a moment and then ducked back to report, "The express is behind us. I can see it." He was wrong: the train he had seen was the second Saugus local.

His overheard remark further upset the apprehensive woman sitting next to Mrs. Story. "There is something wrong about this train," she exclaimed tremulously. "I know something's going to happen."

The next stop was at Everett, the junction for the Saugus branch, and here a ridiculous impasse had developed. According to long-standing Eastern Railroad rules, no northbound train was to move off the main line onto the branch track if a southbound branch train was due and had not yet appeared. This was a reasonable precaution, since the branch line was a single track, but the niggardly railroad had not provided a siding on which an upbound train might await a delinquent opposite number. Instead, it had to stand on the main-line track until the down train appeared.

No serious traffic jam, strange to say, had previously developed at this spot because of the hoary ruling or the lack of a siding, but on August 26th a memorable one built up. The down train from Saugus had been delayed an hour and a half at Lynn for engine repairs. When it finally reached Everett, the first upbound Saugus local; a spare engine, the *Rockport;* the Beverly local; the second upbound Saugus train; and the *Bangor Express* were all strung out in a fuming row along the main northbound track.

"A simple message to the branch trains to meet and pass at any given point other than that in the schedule would have solved the difficulty," wrote Charles Francis Adams, Jr., in his commentary on the absurd situation in *Notes on Railroad Accidents,* published eight years later. "But no!—*there* were the rules, and all of the rolling stock of the road might gather at Everett in solemn procession, but, until the locomotive at Lynn could be repaired, the law of the Medes and the Persians was plain: and in this case it read that the telegraph was a new-fangled and unreliable auxiliary."

There was indeed a telegraph instrument in nearly every Eastern Railroad station, but it was strictly for the use of paying customers. Superintendent Jeremiah Preston, a man to whom progress and change were anathema, had issued orders that the telegraph "machine" was not to be utilized for dispatching trains; he distrusted it. Eastern Railroad trains, like their earliest ancestors, were still run by the timetable.

The snarl at Everett was soon untangled after the tardy downbound Saugus local puffed off the branch line and headed for Boston. The two upbound Saugus trains moved sedately off the main line, and the spare engine, *Rockport*, hitched on to the Beverly local in front of its own engine, *Ironsides*. This was done at the request of the conductor, who said he'd appreciate having the extra motive power to take his train out of the path of the express as soon as possible.

When the switch-tender at Everett finally waved a lantern at Ashbel Brown to let him know that the express was cleared to proceed, Brown thought his way was wide open. He still knew nothing of the Beverly local's presence ahead. "I had no reason to suppose there was another train within six miles of me," he said afterward. Instead, only half that distance away, the Beverly local by now was stopped at the Revere station, which lay at the end of a wide curve.

The express picked up speed briskly as it left the Everett junction. A state constable who watched it pass remarked to a companion, "That train goes like lightning." And John J. Whitcomb, of the Boston *Evening Transcript*, who was headed for the smoker with three male friends, hesitated to cross the open platforms between the swaying Pullman and smoking cars because of the train's rapid progress. "We finally decided to do so," he said, "and hastily scrambled across through the blinding smoke and cinders."

Brown, the engineer, later testified that the train might have been going 25 miles per hour, but no faster. "Suddenly," he recalled, "I discovered two lights looking me in the face." His voice wavered and he broke into tears as he told the story. When he was able to continue, he said, "I immediately reversed my engine and whistled for brakes." Then he jumped from the cab, landing on his face and rolling over and over in the gravel.

John Nolan, conductor of the Beverly local, had just signaled the engineers of *Ironsides* and *Rockport* to move out of the Revere station, when a man on the platform yelled, "Here comes a train!" Nolan swung around to face the oncoming headlight of the *Newburyport*. He jumped to one side and frantically waved his lantern, but the gesture was useless. The express smashed into the rear coach of his train and traveled almost all the way through it.

In the smoker, John Whitcomb, who had been about to sit down, heard the quick whistling for brakes and then, almost simultaneously, "a terrible crash." As he was thrown violently across a seat-back and his friends were hurled to the floor, he saw the front end of the car crumble and move backward in a splintered mass. The kerosene lamps fell and went out. The disarrayed passengers picked themselves up, found they were not injured, and began a panicky struggle to escape. A stern, cool voice checked them. "We're not hurt," a man called out of the darkness. "Let's not be killed by running over each other."

At that, Whitcomb reported, "we passed out orderly and slowly for the platform over which we had just crossed. It had been wrecked . . . and a glance showed that we had escaped maiming and probable death.

"Running quickly forward to learn the cause of the crash," he continued, "first to attract our attention was the seeming absence of the engine of our train in the dense darkness of the night that prevailed. At once a lurid glare burst from the wrecked cars farther along the track, and the awful magnitude of the disaster was revealed. We had struck the rear of a train ahead of us, and our engine had buried itself in one of the cars. . . . The three forward cars of the train were on fire."

The *Newburyport's* stack had been knocked off and its boiler cap sliced away as the engine's momentum carried it through the center of the local's last coach, splitting open the floor and coming to a stop with the roof and dangling sides of the car covering it like a wooden tent. Live steam and boiling water from the wrecked boiler seethed through the debris, scalding many victims trapped between the flanks of the engine and the sides of the car. One passenger miraculously escaped death by being tossed to the top of the rampaging locomotive as if on the horns of a bull, and lying there, pinned in place by the car roof, until rescuers with strong ropes pulled the wreckage off him. His only injury resulted from rolling to the ground when he was suddenly released.

Two cars ahead of the point of impact, "the shock," Charles Story reported, "threw down some who were standing in the aisle, and also threw my child out of my arms. I always supposed that in a collision of this kind the blow came like a thunderclap and was over, but here it was a long, grinding crash, lasting, it seemed to me, fully five seconds.

"Instantaneous with the first sensation the lights were extinguished, and inside the cars it was total darkness. Someone called out, 'The danger is all over—don't be afraid!' The passengers were trampling over one another in their fright and excitement, and I called out the same words. For a second it seemed as if they would have some effect, but the next instant a man near the rear door shouted. 'The car is on fire!' and the excitement was fiercer than ever.

"We all got out at last. My wife had fainted and I laid her on the grass, telling my little girl to stand by her while I helped the others rescue the injured. All the time the air was filled with the shrieks and groans of the wounded and the excited cries of the unhurt passengers and those who happened to be in the vicinity. Men were running about in the greatest excitement, and for a few minutes there was no system of action. . . . Then several gentlemen, residents of Revere and passengers, with more presence of mind than the rest, began to tear off the sides of the car to release the sufferers."

Men ripped the doors off the station to serve as stretchers, and the gathering up of dead and injured took place in the flaring light of the blazing local, its cars having been drawn a few feet up the track and allowed to burn unchecked in order to illuminate the scene and facilitate the rescue work.

Engineer Ashbel Brown, having suffered only scratches and bruises in his leap from the *Newburyport* just before the crash, stumbled up to the wreck and began dazedly trying to find his fireman. In the gush of steam from the broken boiler, he could not at first get close to the ruin of the locomotive and coach. When the steam had dissipated and the car wreckage was removed, Brown looked into the cab and found it empty. The engineer at last encountered his fireman wandering in the crowd, unhurt; he, too, had jumped before the crash. Brown then joined in the relief work and stayed until after midnight.

The casualty list, always subject to confusion and contradiction in the hours immediately following a major disaster, went through several revisions after the Revere wreck. Three days later, however, a carefully rechecked list published in Eastern papers contained the names and home towns of thirty dead and thirty-two injured. The toll was not outstanding among notable railway accidents up to that time, but the wreck at Revere made a devastating impact on the public. In Boston, it was reported that "since the last days of the war there has been no greater commotion in the community." Indignation meetings were held in a dozen Massachusetts cities and towns. Summer residents at Swampscott gathered to hear Wendell Phillips, the former rabid Abolitionist, demand that all railroads henceforth be forced to control the movements of their trains by telegraph.

Here was the basic point of controversy that so stirred the people of the Bay State, who prided themselves on their enlightenment and progressiveness. They were appalled that, a quarter-century after Morse had demonstrated the practicality of the telegraph and two decades after the first railroads had begun using it for dispatching, the Eastern Railroad of Massachusetts was still operating by the timetable. Such backwardness, such inefficiency, was unpardonable. The scandal swelled in volume and pitch when it was revealed that the telegraph was there, all right, but Superintendent Prescott had forbidden his working railroadmen to use it.

In the official investigations that followed the Revere wreck, one of them chaired by Charles Francis Adams, Jr., head of the state Board of Railroad Commissioners, there was no tendency to blame engineers, firemen, or signalmen for the tragedy that occurred on the night of August 26th. Obviously, the top officials of the railroad were primarily to blame for the system that enabled the wreck to take place. Especially clear was the fact that the use of telegraphic dispatching would have prevented the rear-end collision at Revere. Superintendent Prescott was forced to resign; so was President Samuel Browne. Their antiquated railroad was swamped by more than a half-million dollars' worth of damage suits, and eventually lost its corporate identity altogether, being absorbed by the Boston & Maine Railroad in 1884.

7

On the Wildest Night of Winter
(Ashtabula, Ohio: December 29, 1876)

SNOW had been falling without pause for forty-eight hours in northeastern Ohio, and on the evening of December 29, 1876, a gale roaring in across Lake Erie whirled the flakes into flying clouds that reduced visibility to about fifty feet. The temperature was steadily dropping.

Shortly before 7:30 P.M., a quarter-mile east of the little station at Ashtabula, the Lake Shore & Michigan Southern Railroad's *Pacific Express,* bound for Chicago, poked slowly through the curtaining storm and began to cross the double-tracked iron bridge high above Ashtabula Creek. Two locomotives were drawing the eleven-car train, which had left New York City the previous evening. The *Socrates,* in the lead, and the *Columbia* had been laboring through drifts all the afternoon, and the express they were hauling, at about 10 mph, was already three hours behind schedule. The head lamp of the *Socrates* barely illuminated enough of the track ahead to enable its engineer, Daniel McGuire, to tell where he was. In his seventeen years of railroading, McGuire had never experienced worse weather. "It was the wildest winter night of the year," wrote a local newspaper correspondent on the following day.

Behind the locomotives rolled four express and baggage cars, a smoking car, two coaches, a parlor car, and three sleeping cars —*Palatine, City of Buffalo,* and *Osseo*—in that sequence. By the conductor's count, there were one hundred and thirty-one passengers aboard, though some of the passengers who had had a difficult time finding a seat or a berth were convinced that there were far more. The cars were inadequately lighted by lamps containing candles made from sperm oil, and robustly heated by wood stoves in the coaches, patented coal-burning stoves in the parlor car and sleepers. Trains then were commonly overheated and underventilated in winter, but on this particular night, as the blizzard raged against the befogged windows, its frigid winds made themselves felt all too plainly inside, and passengers were in no mood to complain about the stoves.

In *Palatine*, the foremost sleeping car, Captain Charles Tyler, a commission merchant and steamboat owner from St. Louis, had just settled down to a game of casino with three fellow travelers. The first hand had been dealt, but no one had yet played. As the men perused their cards, a ceiling-lamp fixture at the front end of the car suddenly shattered, extinguishing its candles. Tyler had only time to exclaim, "It must be the frost," when the bell-cord broke with a twang, lashing and shattering the two other ceiling lights as it whipped backward. The candles blew out, and in complete darkness the car abruptly dropped forward at a steep angle.

"My God!" shouted one of Tyler's companions. "We're going down!" Instantly, the four men were gripped by the breath-stopping sensation of falling.

Seconds earlier, when the *Socrates* was nearly across the 152-foot bridge, Dan McGuire, with one hand on the throttle, had heard an explosive noise—"like a fog torpedo"—and felt the bridge begin to sink beneath his engine. With a convulsive movement, he pulled the throttle wide open. *Socrates* lunged forward so strongly that it pulled the wheel trucks out from under its tender and broke away from the rest of the train. McGuire glanced behind him in terror and saw *Columbia* rear up and topple backward into the darkness. He failed to hear the grinding uproar of destruction as bridge and train tumbled 75 feet into the steep ravine of frozen Ashtabula Creek, for he was frantically blowing *Socrates*'s whistle and ringing its bell.

Residents of Ashtabula as far away as half a mile had heard the crash, however, even above the moaning wind. That shocking sound, and *Socrates*'s hoots of alarm, brought them and the local fire department to the scene on the run.

First man to reach the bottom of the deeply drifted ravine was Dan McGuire, who had halted his engine as soon as possible and run back to see what help he could give. After wading and sliding down the west bank of the creek, McGuire was astounded and relieved to discover that "Pop" Folsom was alive. The engineer of the *Columbia* was lying at the foot of the slope, not far from his locomotive, which had landed with its wheels in the air. Folsom, bleeding from severe cuts and unable to move because of a broken leg, had been flung out a window of his cab

An artist's conception of the wrecked and burning Pacific Express of the Lake Shore & Michigan Southern Railroad a few minutes after it fell 75 feet into an icy creekbed in the collapse of a double-tracked bridge just east of Ashtabula, Ohio, in a blizzard on the evening of December 29, 1876. This drawing originally appeared in the January 20, 1877, issue of Harper's Weekly.

as it fell. As McGuire bent to lift the injured man out of a snowbank, he said he heard Folsom say, "Another Angola Horror, Dan."

This comment, too apt to be quite believable as having come from a man who must have been dazed and in acute pain, was probably a product of McGuire's imagination. Still, the disaster was unquestionably very similar to the memorable one of December 1867, not many miles east of there. Ashtabula's wreck was on a much greater scale, however. The entire train, except for the leading engine, had fallen into the ravine. Rear cars not yet on the bridge, which was shorter than the train, were pulled to destruction by those ahead, and fires from overturned and broken stoves had blazed up in half a dozen places. Flames, driven by the wind, were already sweeping through the heaped wreckage.

In the plunge of the sleeping car *Palatine,* Captain Tyler and his fellow card players had "sat in breathless suspense for what seemed to me to be ten minutes, it was so agonizing, before we struck the bottom of the ravine." At the coroner's inquest that began on Saturday, December 30th, and continued into the following week, Tyler never again mentioned his companions, and their fate is unknown. The Captain had suffered severe head injuries, and his right hand was lacerated, but on January 1st he was able to appear at the inquest and give a particularly graphic account of what had happened.

"I cannot describe the crash, it was too terrific," he began; but immediately after his own car landed, "the *City of Buffalo* came down sideways and fell on the rear end of our car. It mashed off about ten feet of the end. Two gentlemen had been smoking in that rear section. It was cut entirely off. I think everybody in the *City of Buffalo* was killed by the crash."

Tyler had managed to climb out through a broken window of the *Palatine,* and pulled another survivor, a Miss Shepherd, after him. To get away from the wreck, they had first to clamber over the *City of Buffalo,* which lay on one side across the shattered *Palatine,* in a north–south direction. "It was very difficult to get along it," Tyler said.

"On reaching the south end of the car," he continued, "I hung by my hands to the wreck while Miss Shepherd slid down my body. She went almost out of sight, and I thought she was in water. It was snow, however, very deep. She called out, 'All

right,' and I dropped into the same place. After we got away from the car, fire began to show itself."

The Captain delivered Miss Shepherd into the hands of clustering townspeople and went back to the *Palatine*. He found a man inside, crazed with fright, and had great difficulty in getting him out a window. When that was finally accomplished, the car appeared to be empty.

"The light from the fire was now bright," Tyler recalled. "I was about thirty feet from the west abutment, near the engine, and had a good view of the entire wreck. The baggage and express cars lay by the locomotive, near the west abutment, each lapping one over. The *Palatine* lay almost across the river. The *City of Buffalo* was lying across the rear end of it, due north and south. The cars immediately following these all fell on top of the other in one mashed-up pile, one leaning against the eastern abutment at an angle of forty degrees. [Tyler was a bit confused here. There were not "cars" but only one car, the sleeper *Osseo,* following the *City of Buffalo*. The "mashed-up pile" presumably comprised the smoker, the two coaches, and the parlor car, which had formed the central section of the train, while the car that Tyler saw leaning against the eastern abutment was undoubtedly the *Osseo*.]

"Though many persons were in the *City of Buffalo*," he added, "not a moan came from there." Tyler thought they were all dead, and most of them were.

At least eighty persons died as a result of the fall and subsequent burning of the *Pacific Express* that night. The figure was never more than approximate, and generally thought to be low. Conductor Bernhard Henn, who had been riding in the smoker when the bridge gave way beneath it, had been knocked unconscious in the wreck, and his later recapitulation of the total passenger list was certainly open to question. He had been heard to say just before the wreck that there were one hundred and sixty aboard, not counting children; afterward, he said there had been one hundred and thirty-one passengers. Surviving passengers questioned on this point were unanimous in estimating that there had been at least two hundred people on the train; some placed the total as high as two hundred and fifty. Fifty-two living passengers were helped out of the wreckage or escaped without assistance, though most of them were injured to some degree. As for the rest, the fire was so thorough in its work that an accurate count of the victims was impossible. There was no doubt in anyone's mind then, however, that the wreck at Ashtabula was the deadliest that had occurred since U.S. railroads began running, and they were right.

The crew of the *Pacific Express* was obviously innocent of having been responsible for the wreck in any way. In the two investigations that promptly followed the accident—by a coroner's jury in Ashtabula and by a special joint committee of the Ohio legislature—two principal questions were raised.

The Ashtabula citizens were in a rage over the failure of their fire department to do anything to put out the flames, though two hand-pumpers, a hook-and-ladder, and a steamer had arrived at the edge of the ravine, with five hundred feet of hose, within five minutes after the bridge fell, and a watering station for the railroad, containing a pump with a sixty-pound head of steam, stood at the top of the west bank of the creek, within a hundred feet of the wreck. The coroner's jury, therefore, pri-

According to an artist for Frank Leslie's Illustrated Newspaper *(Jan. 13, 1877), the railroad bridge at Ashtabula looked like this before it fell. The design was that of a conventional Howe truss bridge; the adaptation of that popular and ordinarily dependable design to iron instead of wood was experimental. The experiment was an apparent success for eleven years, but ended in disaster.*

marily sought an answer to why the fire department failed in its basic duty. Its men had helped importantly to assist survivors out of the wrecked cars, but had not put a drop of water on the fires.

The legislature's committee directed its attention to finding out why the bridge collapsed. Was the train too heavy? Had the iron contracted with the cold? Was the bridge overburdened with snow? Had the strong winds toppled both bridge and cars?

Captain Tyler had testified that rescuers flocking to the site of the wreck as he and Miss Shepherd were leaving it hadn't even attempted to throw snow on the flames when the fires started, though it lay all around them in great abundance. Failure of the town firemen to pump water on the blazing wreck had already stimulated vicious rumors to the effect that the railroad's station agent at Ashtabula, Henry Strong, had ordered the fire chief not to do so. The reason, these rumormongers eagerly volunteered, was that the railroad *wanted* the victims to be consumed in the fire, so that no one would ever know how many there were or who they were, and subsequent damage suits would be rendered harmless by this lack of vital evidence. This explanation conveniently ignored the plain fact that the station agent had no authority over the fire department, but it fitted the prevailing mood of the day, which, for copious reasons, was anti-railroad.

The most plausible explanation, brought out in prolonged questioning by counsel before the coroner's jury, appeared to be that the fire chief was a dull-witted and submissive man, and the station agent was somewhat irrational with excitement.

In response to persistent probing, the fire chief, Thomas Knapp, said he had seen Strong, the station agent, at the top of the west embankment when he arrived, and had asked him where he should run his hose. This, of course, was a silly question, since Knapp could have seen for himself. Strong's response, Knapp said, was: "We don't want any water down there, but want help." Knapp took this as an order, though why, he couldn't explain. Strong, in his turn, testified that he hadn't remembered that Knapp had said anything about the hose, but realized he was being asked about putting water on the blaze, and had said impatiently, "I don't want water. I want help." This, he told the jury, was not necessarily meant to dissuade the firemen from fighting the fire but merely reflected his overwhelming feeling at that moment that helping people out of the wreck was much more urgent than putting out the flames. From the present distance in time, Strong's point of view is understandable, though both men should have realized that the work of rescue would be far more effective if the fires were quenched first. As it was, badly injured passengers and those trapped under debris were given no chance to escape, and the subsequent task of identification was vastly complicated, when it was not altogether impossible.

The legislative committee's inquiry into the reasons why the bridge fell involved top officials of the Lake Shore & Michigan Southern Railroad, especially Charles Collins, its chief engineer, and Amasa Stone, formerly its president but at this time a director. Stone was a brother-in-law of William Howe, inventor of the popular Howe truss bridge, a rectangular form consisting of wooden diagonals and vertical iron tie-rods. This bridge had served railroads widely and well so long as it remained predominantly wooden and trains remained relatively light. In 1864, though, Stone decided to adapt the design, to which he by then had exclusive rights, to the use of iron components entirely, and to erect a bridge of this kind over Ashtabula Creek to replace the wooden trestle that then spanned it.

Collins, according to the accounts of others, strongly objected to this experimental approach, which had never been tried before, and recommended building the bridge of stone. The president of the railroad refused; stone would cost at least $18,000 more than iron. Collins disapproved so strongly of the experimental iron bridge that he refused to have anything to do with its construction, leaving that to subordinates. Friends in Cleveland told a reporter after the Ashtabula wreck that Collins had remarked in their hearing that he had never considered the bridge safe. One of them, a fellow engineer, declared that when he had once told Collins that he didn't trust the Ashtabula bridge, Collins had remarked, "If it goes down, I trust it will be with a freight, and not a passenger train."

At the hearings of the legislative committee, Collins denied all these reports, perhaps out of a misguided sense of loyalty to Stone, saying merely that "at about the time the bridge was constructed, I was put on other work." He said he had never looked at the plans for it, and had not seen the bridge at all until requested to do so by a Mr. Rogers, who had completed the installation after its first supervisor had been discharged for inefficiency. Collins discovered that Rogers had the main bracing-beams in wrong, that they had been laid flat, thus weakening the structure, when they should have been stood on edge. Collins, with Stone beside him, had told Rogers to remedy the drastic mistake, and he had done so. At the time, the structure was still resting on scaffolding.

Amasa Stone testified that Rogers had had no previous experience in the erection of iron bridges, "and none since that I know of." He had allowed him to proceed with the Ashtabula bridge, however, after rearranging the braces, because "there could have been no other mistake made." It was Stone's conviction, he told the questioners, that the design of the bridge was not at fault, nor was the use of iron a mistake. What had caused the wreck, he believed, was the derailment of the second locomotive, which had then fallen through the bridge, pulling train and bridge down with it. No one else shared his belief, though, and there was no testimony to support it.

The most revealing testimony about the Ashtabula bridge

came from an interview that a reporter from the Cleveland *Leader* had with an unidentified machinist and bridge-builder of that city who had helped construct it. When the bridge was first in place, on July 1, 1865, and workmen began removing the scaffolding that supported it, the bridge started to settle, this machinist said. Superintendent Rogers was so alarmed that he immediately ordered the men to stop taking out the supports, and called in Collins and other engineers to inspect the job. It was then that Collins had pointed out to him that the braces were improperly installed, and Rogers began the slow, laborious task of repositioning them. At the same time, said the machinist being interviewed, additional braces were installed, four beams being placed where three had been before, five laid where there had been four. Thus, he said, while the bridge was unquestionably made stronger, it was also made heavier. This time, though, when the scaffolding was knocked out, the bridge seemed secure, even when three engines were run onto it at one time—not six, as the story had gone around after the wreck.

The legislative committee sent a team of independent civil engineers to inspect the wrecked bridge and report their conclusions as to why it collapsed. They gave their unanimous opinion, on February 1st, that probably the braces failed first, causing the top chord of the bridge to give way. "Inasmuch as both members were weak and both were involved in the break," they said, "it is of little importance which member took precedence in the failure." They added, "The factors of safety throughout the compression members were so low that failure must have followed sooner or later at this point." In conclusion, the engineers said they had found nothing to justify "the popular apprehension that there may be some inherent defect in iron as a material for bridges." On the other hand, "the failure of the Ashtabula bridge could have been prevented at a moderate cost." The wonder, truly, was why it had stood as long as it had.

At the conclusion of the legislative committee's hearings, no criminal charges were brought against either Stone or Collins, but each man in time passed judgment upon himself.

Two days after testifying before the committee, Collins, whose family was away on a visit, was found lying dead on his bed, a bullet wound in his skull. His right hand clutched a revolver. A second revolver and a razor lay within reach of his left hand. He had been dead for twenty-four hours.

Five years later, Amasa Stone, who had been in delicate health at the time of the wreck, also committed suicide.

The most important result of the Ashtabula tragedy, which stirred the nation profoundly, was that it led Representative James A. Garfield, of Ohio, the minority leader in the House, to introduce a bill in Congress that would set up a committee of three members of the Army Corps of Engineers to investigate and report on every railway accident involving loss of life, with the purpose of determining the causes and suggesting preventives. The future President's bill was written largely by Charles Francis Adams, Jr., grandson of former President John Quincy Adams, who had been in the first U.S. railway accident that killed passengers.

This bill was the nucleus of the provisions for reporting, investigating, and preventing accidents that eventually were incorporated in the Interstate Commerce Act of 1887, and strengthened in its many subsequent revisions. Previously, individual states had tried in their own, mainly ineffectual, ways to curb railway accidents. Here, at last, was the beginning of the first national effort to put a stop to the needless slaughter.

8

A Runaway in the Mountains
(Tehachapi, California: January 20, 1883)

IN the wilder days of the West, early in the year 1883, when it was not at all uncommon for passenger trains in lonely regions to be held up and robbed by masked bandits, a particularly terrifying accident occurred on the Southern Pacific Railroad in southern California. It was the kind of accident most feared by nervous railroad travelers of the time: a high-speed runaway in the mountains, ending in a flaming crash as stoves and kerosene kindled the inevitable fire in the wreckage. Briefly, but mistakenly, the disaster was purported to have been staged by would-be robbers.

The accident took place in the Tehachapi Mountains. Between California's great agricultural central valley and its high Mojave Desert, a Southern Pacific train bound for Los Angeles on the railroad's San Joaquin Valley route must climb over a pass in those mountains. The rise is from 2,734 feet at the western base of the range to 4,025 feet at the summit. It encompasses 28 miles of track, numerous tunnels, and the celebrated figure-8 of the Tehachapi Loop, one of the marvels of 19th Century railroading and still an object of admiration among connoisseurs of engineering feats. The ascending coils of the Loop lie ten miles below the summit. From there to the top of the pass, the road follows a sinuous course along mountain shelves and through gorges at a gradient made less taxing by the ingenious Loop but still commanding respect and special locomotive exertion. In 1883, the Loop was only seven years old, and the grade in some places above it was even steeper than it is now. Not far below the summit, it was 129 feet to the mile.

Shortly after midnight on January 20th of that year, the SP's *Overland Express,* en route from San Francisco to Los Angeles, halted at Sumner, at the foot of the long climb, to pick up an extra engine to help it get to the summit. The train was made up

The flaming end of the Southern Pacific's runaway Overland Express, after its derailment on the Tehachapi Grade at 70–75 mph on the frosty night of January 19, 1883, is depicted by an artist for Frank Leslie's Illustrated Newspaper.

of two baggage cars, a mail-and-express car, two Pullman sleepers, a smoker, and a coach. There were between sixty and seventy persons aboard, including twenty Chinese track laborers riding in the smoker and nearly that many passengers in the coach, at the tail end of the train. The helper engine was cut into the consist between the regular engine and the first baggage car. In this awkward arrangement lay the seeds of disaster. It seems odd that the helper engine did not hook on in front, but probably it was less powerful than the other locomotive. In any event, once the train had huffed up to Tehachapi Summit, both engines had to be uncoupled in order to permit the helper to return home, and in the course of that maneuver a fatal mistake was made.

The night was extremely cold and windy. Winter weather in southern California is usually benign beside the sea, but at higher altitudes it often rivals the severe climate of much more northerly regions. At Tehachapi Summit, only a few nights earlier, a temperature of 20 degrees below zero had been reported. On this Saturday, when the *Overland Express* arrived at the summit, a frigid wind of near-gale strength was buffeting the pass with violent gusts, and the temperature was so low that water quickly froze when exposed to it.

Passengers on the express were mostly asleep in the stuffy warmth generated by coal stoves when the train creaked to a straining stop on frost-coated rails outside the summit station. Among those in the Pullmans were a former Governor of California, John G. Downey, and his wife; railroad magnate Charles Crocker's daughter Amy and her young husband, Richard Porter Ashe; and Howard Tilton, general freight agent of the Canadian Pacific Railway, who was on his way to Washington, D. C. Mrs. Downey, a member of one of the old land-holding Spanish families of earlier California, was terrified of trains. She had previously vowed never to ride in one again, and was on the *Overland Express* this night only because the Governor had been more than usually persuasive and because Los Angeles was home. Amy Crocker Ashe and her husband had been married secretly a month before, in defiance of Amy's mother, who had arranged her engagement to a prosperous London businessman the previous summer. When the Crockers came home to Sacramento after their Grand Tour, however, Amy had promptly fallen in love with Porter Ashe, a law clerk, and they had eloped. Maternal tears and recriminations were now past, and the Ashes were openly celebrating their honeymoon, with benefit of parental blessings and an attending maid for the bride. Porter Ashe was also enjoying the unaccustomed satisfaction of carrying $1,700 in greenbacks—though not for long, for the money was lost in the wreck that soon followed.

When the express pulled in to the Tehachapi station, at about 2:30 A.M., G. H. McKenzie, a former brakeman who had found it impossible to sleep sitting up in the coach, was standing on the front platform of the smoking car, chatting with the conductor. The latter then stepped off, swinging a lantern from his right hand, and walked into the station to report the time of arrival of his train, as he was required to do. The forward brakeman was busy up front, helping with the uncoupling of the engines and manning the turntable, so that the helper could head back for Sumner.

At this moment, McKenzie was surprised to hear voices and see the rear brakeman escorting a young woman passenger from the coach toward the station. "Isn't there a hotel in this place?" the woman asked her companion as they passed McKenzie. "Yes," the brakeman replied, "but I'll show you into the office."

McKenzie remembered enough of his railroading experience to realize that the brakeman was not supposed to leave his post except in an emergency, and he was certain that the railroad rule-makers hadn't envisioned this obvious situation as an emergency requiring the brakeman's intervention. Still, he was no more than mildly curious at the infraction of rules. Very soon after entering the station, the brakeman reappeared. He had not walked very far against the pummeling wind, however, before his lantern blew out, and he turned back into the station to re-light it.

Almost simultaneously, the cars began to move slowly backward. McKenzie, who could not see the head of the train while the cars were strung out in a straight line, assumed that the express was being backed onto a siding. He was unperturbed until he noticed that the smoker was passing the siding switch and was still on the main track. Furthermore, the train was traveling faster by the moment. At this point, the track curved enough so that McKenzie, by leaning far out from the platform, could see that there was no engine at the front end of the train.

Instantly realizing that the train was running away, with no brakemen on it, McKenzie grabbed the wheel of the hand brake on the front platform of the smoker. He couldn't budge it. So he jumped across to the rear platform of the second sleeping car and tried working the brake there. This time, he was partly successful, but his efforts did not seem to be retarding the train an inch. He then grabbed the knob of the sleeper's rear door, only to discover that the door was locked. Desperately, McKenzie turned and ran back through the smoker to its rear platform. He found he could make the brake there take hold, but by this time the train was rolling backward down the mountain at frightening speed, the cars rocking dizzily as they reeled around the curves.

"How fast did we go down hill?" said A. R. McCall, the mail agent, to a San Francisco reporter in later describing the wild dash. "Well, I have ridden fifty and sixty miles an hour, but I'll be blessed if this didn't beat anything in the way of speed I ever saw or dreamed of. To say seventy miles an hour is to put it at the lowest estimate."

McKenzie meanwhile had rushed back to the forward end of the smoker, to try once more to make the brake there take hold. He was joined by another passenger, Stephen Coffyn.

Just then, as the cars screeched around a curve on top of a 15-foot embankment, the coupling between the smoker and the second sleeper broke. The uphill portion of the train cascaded off the track to its right and landed in a crunching heap, the thunder of its destruction reverberating through the hills and attracting nearby ranchers to the scene. The liberated smoker and coach, still clinging together, raced on down toward the Loop. They got only a couple of miles farther, though, before they were brought to a stop by men who by then were clinging for dear life to all four hand brakes.

Howard Tilton, the Canadian Pacific's general freight agent, who had been dozing in his lower berth on the left-hand side of the first sleeper, was awakened by the rocking of the car and the roar of increasing speed. Having jerked up the window curtain to see what was happening, and immediately realizing his acute peril, he "lay down again to wait for the inevitable, with the feeling that a man must experience when he is standing on a scaffold in expectation of the fall of the trap."

Tilton described his adventures to a reporter for the San Francisco *Call* when he eventually got back to that city. He was a mature, experienced railroadman, whose unembellished account of what happened has the sound of truth:

It seemed only an instant when the crash came [Tilton recalled], and I was hurled from my berth. I had been sleeping on the left side of the car, which fell upon its right side, and I was covered to my waist with mattresses, woodwork, and debris, but found no difficulty in freeing myself.

Smoke passed through the car, giving timely token of the impending peril.

To the right and rear, I saw Mr. and Mrs. Porter Ashe perfectly free, but Miss Petersen, the maid, was buried under about six feet of debris, on the top of which was a water cooler and wash basin. Mrs. Ashe was endeavoring to extricate her, and I assisted in clearing away the rubbish. We soon succeeded in pulling her out.

They were the only persons in sight. I pushed up the window on what was then the top of the car and found it to work perfectly, not a pane having been cracked. I crawled through and drew Miss Petersen out, and Mrs. Ashe followed. I asked Porter Ashe to throw out some blankets, which he did, and then crawled through himself. . . . The cold was intense, and we shivered even though wrapped in blankets. Deep stillness followed the crash, and we heard only one scream while we were in the car.

As I emerged from the car, I saw Mr. Hatch and his mother climbing out of another window. I ran along and found we could reach the ground by means of the platform. I lowered Miss Petersen, Mr. and Mrs. Ashe leaping to the ground.

If there is a small gleam of humor to be found in this grim story, it lies in the contrast between Tilton's laconic account and Porter Ashe's dramatically enhanced version of the same sequence of action, with himself in the starring role. Unfortunately for Ashe, both accounts were printed in the same newspaper, on the same day.

Our maid was buried in the debris [the bridegroom said], my wife and I falling on top of her. The car immediately took fire, and we were forced to take the timber and burning boards off the maid piece by piece. The car became enveloped in smoke. By breaking the windows at the top of the car, I succeeded in rescuing my wife and maid and pushed them through the window.

We were climbing off the car, nearly suffocated by the smoke, when I heard a man calling for help and beseeching us not to leave him. I reached down through a broken window and succeeded in getting hold of Governor Downey's hand and pulling him out, nearly strangled.

While helping her maid to the ground, my wife stepped on the window and fell through into the car again. The car by this time was burning rapidly. It is impossible to tell how I got her out. I jumped with her to the ground and immediately ran down the hill to avoid the flames.

Young Ashe, though thoroughly conscious of what was expected of him as the recently acknowledged husband of one of the state's best-known heiresses, did not forget to mention his supporting cast. "Mr. Howard Tilton," he said, "rendered us great assistance and acted splendidly."

The upper part of the car by this time was in flames [Tilton's version of the story continued]. Passing along by the sleeper, I saw the legs of a man protruding from the car. He was piteously calling for help. I succeeded in partially extricating him, when a train man came to my assistance, and we saved him from a horrible death. He proved to be John F. Cassell of San Francisco [whose wife had been instantly killed in the crash], and he was the last person taken alive from the ruins. All human efforts were of no further avail, as the sleeper was in a sheet of flames.

We left the spot and limped down to the bottom of the ravine, some fifty feet below, where we found ex-Governor Downey, Mr. Cassell, Mr. and Mrs. Ashe, Miss Petersen, Captain Waterhouse and his daughter, and a few other persons scattered about, shivering in the cold blast. Among the rocks on the steep side of the slope lay Wright, the porter, wounded to death and begging for help. . . . I attempted to assist Wright, who was dying, but, being worn out, I could do but little.

A brakeman named McKenzie did all in his power for us.

As soon as the smoker and the coach had been brought to a halt, two miles below the wreck, McKenzie had shouted to the passengers to get out at once, and they scrambled to obey. He naturally expected the rest of the train to come roaring down upon them, at any instant. Instead, there was a strange silence. Then he noticed a flickering light on the slopes up toward the summit, and realized that the other cars had been wrecked and were ablaze. Asking one man to remain behind with the women passengers, McKenzie called to the other men to follow him, and off they went up the track at a run.

When he reached the suffering survivors at the bottom of the ravine where they had crept to get away from the blazing cars, McKenzie said some were crying for water. "I could find no vessel to carry it in," he said, "so I took my hat and got some from the creek. But before I could get it to the sufferers, it was almost frozen solid."

Before long, the helper engine came down the mountain with five or six flatcars, and on these were loaded the handful of survivors from the Pullmans and the baggage and mail cars, together with the able-bodied passengers who had come up from the coach and smoker. The smoker and coach passengers left behind were retrieved later.

Thirteen persons, the majority of Pullman passengers, had died in the wreck, but the total toll was fifteen. The porter survived for only an hour or two, and another of the critically injured passengers died in a Los Angeles hospital a few days afterward.

Mrs. John Downey, who had so dreaded taking this trip, had perished, and so had the single woman whose scream Howard Tilton and the Ashes had heard. John Cassell had been trying to crawl out of the wreck when he heard her, too, and he had been close enough to ask if she was hurt. She said she wasn't, but she was trapped. Cassell couldn't reach her; he couldn't even save his wife; and by the time Tilton hauled him out of a top window of the overturned car, no one else could reach the trapped woman either.

Two days after the disaster on the Tehachapi grade, a masked gang held up a Central Pacific passenger train in the desolate reaches of the Nevada desert near Montello. Hardly had this news been printed when a mysterious and melodramatic new interpretation of the Tehachapi wreck appeared in the papers. There were two victims of that wreck whom nobody could identify, and the story went around that they were would-be robbers who had released the brakes on the *Overland Express* in the expectation of letting the train roll down out of sight of the summit station, then stopping it and stealing the passengers' money, "as well as two boxes of treasure that were in an iron safe in the express car." Instead, the train had got away from them, and they, quite appropriately, had been killed in the ensuing wreck.

Not many readers were inclined to believe this yarn, and McKenzie, former Governor Downey, and Stephen Coffyn all wrote letters to editors declaring that they didn't believe a word of it. There was no substantiation, and the story quickly disappeared from the press after the San Francisco *Chronicle* declared that it had no doubt but that the Central Pacific robbery had inspired "the gauzy story cooked up by the railroad attorneys to induce sufferers to abate their claims for damages."

F. W. Dougherty, a Southern Pacific route agent who had been riding in the mail car of the *Overland Express* when it ran away, told a *Chronicle* reporter, "This accident is the grossest case of criminal neglect I have ever seen or heard of."

It took another Southern Pacific locomotive engineer, though, to explain what unquestionably caused the runaway. The engineer, who prudently refrained from revealing his name to the *Chronicle,* said:

> When we stop a train on a grade, we invariably fill the pipe [compressed-air hose] with air, especially when we intend uncoupling the engine. This keeps the train stationary, and would on the steepest of grades. Even were the track slippery, it would keep it from going very far. When the air brakes are used, the hand brakes are never set, and it is my opinion that they were not in this case. I am convinced that in uncoupling the engine, the engineer forgot to force the air into the pipes, or, if he did so to bring the train to a stop, drew it off again before they were unhitched. But I will allow, for the sake of argument, that the hand brakes were set. The release of air would then change the position of the wheels and make the hand brakes perfectly loose, and consequently useless until properly tightened. It has been proved a fact, however, that the brakemen who should attend to this were not on the train, and consequently there was nobody to attend to the work.
>
> My opinion [this undoubted authority concluded] is that the engineer thoughtlessly let out the air from the tube, this being the custom when the train is brought to a stop on the level, and this disaster was the result.

If this was, indeed, the final judgment on the cause of the wreck, it never reached the newspapers. A coroner's jury at Bakersfield found that the accident had occurred "by reason of the negligence of Conductor B. F. Reid and Brakeman Patten," he who had so gallantly been conducting a young woman to the nearest ladies' room when the train slipped away from the summit station in the windy darkness. The men were not prosecuted, however.

The true reason for the disaster on the Tehachapi grade was the oldest in railroading: human failure. It must, however, have taught a lasting lesson not only to Southern Pacific engineers and those who made the operating rules for them but to engineers of all American railroads that cross mountains, for the impressive fact is that since that January night in 1883 there has never been another major accident involving a runaway passenger train on any Class I U.S. railroad.

9

Disaster at the White River Bridge
(Near West Hartford, Vermont: February 5, 1887)

EARLY in the evening of February 4, 1887, Clarence Hutchinson, a trackwalker for the Central Vermont Railroad, had set out from White River Junction well padded against the bitter cold and had tramped northwestward over the ties for more than four miles before turning back. The snowy countryside was bright with moonlight. The wind blew sharply out of the north, ruffling the dark spruces, dusting the white slopes. The temperature was close to 20 degrees below zero.

Hutchinson's solitary patrol was part of his daily stint in helping to carry out the railroad's policy of having its entire track inspected every twenty-four hours. Many other CV trackwalkers, elsewhere along the line, shared in the lonely vigil.

Hutchinson, holding his lantern low so that he could see the rails well, had walked out along one side of the single track and back down the other. As he was trained to do, he had paid particular attention to the condition of the rails on curves, especially along the slightly winding eastern approach to the 640-foot, stone-piered, four-span wooden deck-bridge across the White River, four miles northwest of the Junction. Hutchinson made his way across the ice-slick bridge and three-quarters of a mile beyond it before returning. He found nothing wrong with the track at any point, and by eleven o'clock was home in bed, decidedly grateful to be there. He was asleep long before the northbound *Montreal Express,* running an hour and a half late that night, clattered past his house on its way to the White River bridge. A neighbor of Hutchinson's, sitting up with a sick child, said later that he had never heard the express go by so fast before. His testimony seems to have been largely imaginative. It was disputed by an overwhelming number of witnesses, among both passengers and train crew, who agreed that the train was traveling at its usual 25-to-30-mph pace before it got to the bridge.

The *Montreal Express,* consisting of one section from Boston

The combined drawing of the blazing wreck of the Montreal Express
*and the ruins of the White River Bridge with its burning cars set afire
and derailed after they fell from it in the early morning of February 5,
1887, appeared in* Harper's Weekly *two weeks later. The main view
was based on a photo taken later the same day from the opposite bank
of the river, toward which the* Express *was moving when it was derailed.*

and another from New York, the latter coming up through Springfield over the track of the Connecticut River Railroad, made up nightly in White River Junction and was normally ready to depart by the scheduled time, 12:40 A.M.

On Friday evening, February 4th, the Springfield section—a coach and the Pullman sleeping car *St. Albans*—had been greatly delayed. As a result, it was not until 2:10 on Saturday morning that the express, with the Springfield section inserted between the Boston coach and the Boston sleeper, *Pilgrim,* moved out for Montreal. The train was hauled by the 45-ton locomotive *E. H. Baker,* with Charles H. Pierce, an engineer of nineteen years' experience, at the controls. Behind the tender strung a baggage car, a combined mail car and smoker, and the four passenger cars, whose coal stoves the trainmen had freshly stoked to ward off the penetrating chill. There were nearly ninety persons aboard, including the train crew of twelve. Many of the passengers were bound for Montreal's annual winter carnival. Some of them, especially in the second coach, were already anticipating the mood of that event.

Because the train was so late, three persons boarded it at White River Junction who had had no previous intention of doing so. Two of them were popular Dartmouth sophomores and roommates, Edward Dillon, a pitcher for the college baseball team, and Albin Veazey, a Rutland judge's son. The boys had been attending a dance at the Junction. When they came out of the hall, well after midnight, and saw the *Montreal Express* still standing in the station, they decided on impulse not to return to Hanover but instead to take the train to Burlington for an impromptu weekend with friends who lived there.

The third passenger who hadn't intended to be aboard the express that night was Henry W. Tewksbury, a middle-aged lecturer of statewide reputation, who had spent earlier hours of the evening describing the Battle of Gettysburg to an audience in Windsor, a few miles south of the Junction. Among his most attentive listeners had been Smith Sturtevant, a forty-one-year-old Civil War veteran and long-time employee of the Central Vermont Railroad. Tonight, Sturtevant was scheduled to be conductor of the *Montreal Express* from the Junction north. After the lecture, he and Tewksbury, old friends, rode the tardy Springfield section together from Windsor to the Junction. There they parted, for the weary lecturer had decided to spend the night at

A more distant photograph of the White River wreck scene, undoubtedly by the same photographer, shows a huge crowd of curious bystanders strung across the ice covered river beside the burned remains of train and bridge. At right, if you have a magnifying glass, you can discern a dense gathering of sleighs; Oscar Paine's farmhouse, where many of the injured were treated; and, on the top of the railroad embankment beyond it, the solitary mail car of the Montreal Express, which the train's fireman hauled out of danger just after the bridge caught fire.

the Junction House, where he had often stayed before. This time, with fateful results for him, Tewksbury was turned away. The hotel was full, and he was obliged to trudge back to the train, expecting to complete his homeward journey on it. He lived in West Randolph, about thirty miles north of White River Junction.

Tewksbury found an empty seat at the front end of the first coach. This fortuitous choice probably saved his life. When he saw Conductor Sturtevant moving down the car aisle toward him to begin collecting tickets, Tewksbury pulled out his watch and noted the time. It was 2:18 a.m. The train had begun to slow down as it swung around the curve onto the White River bridge. It was about to cross the river.

When the conductor saw who was sitting in the front seat of the first coach, he broke into a derisive laugh. As Tewksbury handed up his ticket to be punched, Sturtevant jollied him about not being sound asleep and snoring in the Junction House by now.

At the same time, in the Springfield sleeper, Dillon and Veazey were preparing for bed. Studentlike, they had decided to conserve their funds for the weekend by sharing a lower berth. They were in it now, in the awkwardly constricted process of undressing.

"Suddenly," Tewksbury recalled afterward, "we felt a swaying of the car back and forth, and a jolting, and I knew the wheels were running on the sleepers [ties]. I jumped to pull the bell-cord, and at the same time Mr. Sturtevant did the same. He gave it three long pulls and held it down the last time."

George Parker, one of the brakemen, had been tending to the fire in the stove at the rear of the first coach when the violent jouncing started. He remembered hearing someone—he thought it was Sturtevant—shout, "For God's sake, what's the matter?"

Parker grabbed his lantern and sprang out onto the rear platform. Looking back, he could see sparks flying from the under parts of the following cars, "as if they were off the track and being struck by the wheels." A frantic glance in the other direction showed him the ice-covered river immediately ahead. His part of the train was about to enter upon the bridge, which had no guardrails.

Parker promptly jumped off the train, still clutching his lantern.

"We were going only about seven miles an hour," he said,

though he was quite low in his estimate, "and I thought that I should land all right on my feet." He did; however, he was briefly stunned and his lantern was blown out as he fell in deep snow to the left of the bridge and slid down the bank all the way to the river.

In the cab of the locomotive, now halfway across the bridge, Engineer Pierce heard the alarm bell ring but once. That was enough. "It sounded between stations, so I knew it meant danger," he said afterward. He applied the air brakes instinctively, looking backward out the open window beside him as he did so. The sight was blood-chilling, for he saw most of his train lurch off the track, turn over, and crash upside down on the river's thick ice, 42 feet below.

"I saw the hind end of the Boston sleeper swinging off the bridge to the right," he said. "As that went off, it pulled the Springfield sleeper, then the Springfield coach, and then the Boston coach." The last, directly behind the mail car, was wrenched off its front trucks. The coupling snapped between it and the mail car, enabling the forward end of the train to escape the chain disaster. As the locomotive screeched to a stop, only the rear half of the mail car still rested on the bridge.

The derailed cars collapsed on impact, their heavy wheel trucks and frames adding their crushing weight to the splintered wreckage of the wooden sides and roofs.

As the Springfield sleeper jolted off the rails onto the ties, Edward Dillon jumped out of the berth he was occupying with his friend Veazey. The latter stayed behind, clinging desperately to the swaying sides.

"I remember being thrown first to one side and then the other," Veazey said the next day, "and to have a feeling that we were falling. Then the car, bottom up, struck the ice with a tremendous crash."

Veazey, pinned down by debris, found himself lying full length on the ceiling of the bottom berth.

"Ed," he yelled, "are you hurt?"

Dillon answered in a weak voice, from a location that Veazey could not determine, that he was badly hurt. That was the last time Veazey ever heard him speak.

Veazey struggled to free himself. He felt something give way beneath his legs, and discovered that he could wriggle out backward into the subzero night. He was clad only in his underwear, but the smashed stoves in all four cars had already set the wreckage afire, and the heat of the rapidly spreading flames, together with his distracted excitement, kept him from being aware of the encircling cold. Searching through the wreckage in a frenzy, Veazey found a train ax and began hacking at the remains of the car, calling repeatedly to Dillon. He no longer could distinguish his friend's voice among the moans and screams of the injured and trapped. Fierce heat and thick smoke soon drove him back.

When Engineer Pierce had brought the forward end of the train to a stop, he and his fireman, together with the baggagemaster, the expressman, and two mail agents, grabbed shovels and axes, slid down the steep, slippery west bank of the river, and ran out across the ice to rescue as many passengers as they could. Veazey, having been forced to give up his lone battle to save Dillon, joined them.

The impact of the falling train had not broken the strong ice over the river. Therefore, survivors and families of the victims did not, as a commentator rather delicately expressed it a few days later, "even have the relief of believing that many were drowned before the flames reached them."

One of the first persons extricated from the wreck was Henry Tewksbury, who afterward described his singularly harrowing experience.

"I was stunned for a moment by the terrible crash," he said, "and hardly knew whether I was dead or alive. I tried to move, but couldn't budge an inch. I struggled with all my strength to free myself, screaming for help, but there was no one at hand to help me."

Tewksbury saw fire break out at the far end of his car, and watched in agony as the flames and smoke spread toward him.

"It was a time of mental torture," he said, "but I still could not help noticing an old couple who had sat a few seats behind me. They were hopelessly tied down by heavy seats, and the flames were approaching them with frightful rapidity. I could do nothing for them. Before the smoke shut them from sight, I saw them locked in each other's arms."

Tewksbury, giving himself up for lost, pulled his fur cap down over his eyes "to hide the dreadful view of approaching death."

At that moment he heard voices. Snatching off his cap, he saw the engineer and fireman a few feet away. He yelled to them for help.

"I heard Engineer Pierce say to his fireman, 'Take hold! Perhaps we can save Tewksbury,' " the lecturer recalled. "They are two powerful men, and they both braced themselves by putting their feet against the car, and pulled with all their strength. Still they could not move me, and said they must leave me.

" 'Don't! Don't!' " I cried. " 'Try, for God's sake, to save me. Try again!'

"They did so, and with the same result. They said it was no use. I begged them to try once more—to pull my leg off if they had to, but not let me burn. They pulled—and, oh, with what a joyous feeling did I feel my feet gradually slipping from my shoes. I cried out that I was moving—to pull, pull, pull! I felt one of my legs break, but I was released. To do it, they had to haul me over the debris by the collar.

"They dropped me on the ice by the side of the burning car, and within two feet of it," Tewksbury continued. "I said, 'Draw me back farther—I shall burn here.' They did so, pulling me back twenty-five feet or more—right under the bridge.'

This move merely increased his peril, though none of them realized it at the moment. His rescuers left him to save others. Through a shattered window of the first car, they saw Conductor Sturtevant creeping feebly along, the clothes on his back ablaze. They threw a shovelful of snow on him in an effort to put out the flames. The attempt failed, but they soon managed to haul him out through another broken window and quench the fire. Sturtevant was nearly naked and severely burned. Handling him as gently as they could, two members of the train crew began carrying him toward Oscar Paine's farmhouse, at the top of the west bank of the river. He died a few hours later.

Tewksbury watched them go with rising alarm. By this time, long tongues of flame from the burning cars had licked the lower timbers of the bridge and set them smoldering. Blazing embers shortly began to shred onto the ice near the helpless lecturer, suffering, he had discovered, from a broken arm as well as a broken leg. He lay there trembling with cold and shock, and in terror of having the bridge fall down upon him.

Engineer Pierce, noting at this moment that the structure was afire, sent his fireman scrambling up the icy bank to move the engine forward and draw the mail car out of danger. With another member of his crew, Pierce then resumed lugging Sturtevant toward the Paine farmhouse.

"I begged them to take me," Tewksbury said, "but they told me they must take Sturtevant there first, as he was suffering a good deal."

Tewksbury saw them clamber up the slope, falling several times in their efforts.

Not far away from him lay Mrs. W. S. Bryden, of Montreal, wrapped in a blanket that a dazed survivor had gathered around her as he helped her out of the wreckage, her clothes torn off in her previous struggles to free herself. She was too badly injured to walk, and choked by smoke. Her rescuer had dropped her in the snow, in the midst of a bizarre scattering of oranges and bananas that had cascaded from the buffet section of one of the sleepers as it fell. The man had put Mrs. Bryden down within a few feet of the blazing cars and, she related hysterically, had then handed her an orange, saying, "Here, eat this. It's good for you."

"From the car," she went on, "I could hear the most terrible cries, piercing my soul. One voice still rings in my ears. It was that of another woman, who kept crying, 'Won't someone let me out?' "

At about this time, young Veazey, having been forced to give up trying to rescue Dillon, came along and found a stray berth mattress for Mrs. Bryden. He eased her onto it and dragged her back to a safe distance from the fire, which was threatening to blister her feet.

Tewksbury's rescue party was back within fifteen minutes after delivering Sturtevant to where he could get more solicitous attention. They were pushing a sled, and so exhausted that they sprawled on the ice, gasping for breath, before they recovered enough strength to move him. They were all back inside the Paine farmhouse, however, when the bridge fell. They heard the thudding of its collapse.

Meanwhile, George Parker, the brakeman who had jumped from the train in order to escape the wreck, had roused a farmer who lived near the eastern end of the bridge. Together they threw harnesses on a team of horses and galloped off toward the Junction to spread the alarm and bring additional help.

A trainload of relief forces, including several doctors routed from bed, came roaring up from the Junction within three-quarters of an hour after the express overturned. By then, there was nothing left of the four fallen passenger cars but smoking heaps of charred wood and twisted iron. Only the stone piers of the bridge remained.

One of the luckiest passengers on the *Montreal Express* that night was Henry Mott, of Alburg, Vermont. He boarded the northbound Springfield section of the train at Bellows Falls, fell heavily to sleep in his berth in the *St. Albans,* was knocked unconscious in his sleep when the wreck occurred, and knew nothing at all about the calamity until he came to in a hotel room in White River Junction on Saturday afternoon.

By nightfall on February 5th, all New England had heard about the disaster, in which thirty-four persons had died and forty-nine others were hurt.

Before curious crowds had had time to congregate on the banks and surface of the White River and stare at the blackened wreckage, Professor Robert Fletcher, noted director of Dartmouth's Thayer School of Civil Engineering, visited the location. It was about noon on Saturday, ten hours after the wreck. He and a few of his students inspected the track along the eastern approach to the river. They found that new rails had already been laid for about 450 to 470 feet back from the edge. This had been done as quickly as possible that morning, CVRR officials subsequently testified, to enable relief trains to move close to the river. The tracklayers had not bothered to take away the replaced rails, merely tossing them into the snow beside the rebuilt track. There, Thayer and his students found fragments of broken rails that showed unmistakable evidence of extensive internal flaws. One long piece of rail bore the stamp "St. Albans, 1881." This provided the most graphic evidence of internal flawing. Railroad officers said later that that particular rail had been rolled in their St. Albans shops from unfinished steel imported from Scotland, and had been laid the same year it was rolled. It had somehow managed to stay intact in all weathers for six years.

Professor Fletcher, in a requested report to *Engineering News* three days after the wreck, expressed his astonishment at that fact. "Indeed it is difficult to understand," he wrote, "how such a rail could have allowed the passage of a locomotive a dozen times without fracture."

Vermont's State Railroad Commission, which began its investigation of the causes of the wreck on Saturday afternoon, about twelve hours after it happened, came to the official conclusion that the rail that broke under the weight of the train in the extreme cold of early morning on February 5th had indeed been primarily responsible for the accident. The commissioners declared that the broken rail had thrown the passenger cars off the track before they reached the bridge, and that thumping over the ties had snapped one car axle, whose halves were discovered lying on opposite sides of the bridge in the snow blanket covering the river's ice. This triggered the fall of the four cars.

The commission found also that "the defect in the rail could not have been discovered before it broke." [Professor Fletcher confirmed that fact, and, indeed, there did not exist at that time any technological means of detecting internal flaws in metal, as X-rays routinely do today.] Furthermore, the commission declared that the train had properly slowed up as it approached the bridge, and "there was no culpable negligence on the part of the railroad company."

"There is no doubt, however," the commissioners concluded, "that many who lost their lives in the accident would have been saved if it had not been for the stoves and lights in the wrecked cars."

It was this obvious truth that particularly roused public indignation. There was a widespread feeling of deep outrage that while safe methods of heating and lighting railroad cars—steam and electricity—existed and were already being adopted by a few progressive lines, most train travelers were still at the mercy of archaic and dangerous conditions of transportation. In the advanced year of 1887, more than a half-century after the first U.S. train ran, this was considered to be an intolerable situation. Many a legislator in state capitals and in Washington rose to view with alarm what happened in Vermont on the frigid night of February 5, 1887. Within five years after the disaster at the White River bridge the first national legislation establishing safety standards for railroad equipment came into being: the Railway Appliances Act of 1893. In a very short time thereafter, the annual toll of railroad accidents dropped by more than 60 percent.

10

Fire in the Grass
(Chatsworth, Illinois: August 10, 1887)

TIM COUGHLAN and four of his section hands had been burning dry grass all the long, torrid August afternoon. They were working beside the track of the Toledo, Peoria & Western Railroad along a six-mile sector between Chatsworth and Piper City, in east-central Illinois. The empty prairie that spread to the horizon around them like the top of a table was baked hard from a weeks-long drought. Burning the tall, reedy grass that flanked the roadbed and fringed the withered stream channels that crossed it beneath wooden culverts was a sensible precaution. Sparks from passing locomotives had set this standing hay ablaze in several places along the line in recent months. In at least a couple of instances, the creeping flames had ignited bridges. The fires had been noticed and put out, however, before they could cause serious damage—until August 10, 1887.

Shortly before four o'clock on that Wednesday afternoon, a slow freight moved eastward toward Coughlan's gang. From its rear platform, Roadmaster Christopher Ennis leaned far out to get a better view of the receding track. He was under special orders to inspect roadbed and bridges today in advance of a big excursion train that would be passing over the line during the evening en route to Niagara Falls. A half-mile west of the grass-burners, Ennis took particular note of a small culvert situated about halfway between Chatsworth and Piper City. The culvert was 15 feet long and stood 6 feet above a gully that in spring had held a thread of water but now was as dry as the prairie. Ennis saw nothing wrong with the little bridge, and waved casually to Coughlan's gang as he rode through the heat and smoke of their carefully controlled fires half a mile beyond it.

The freight was the last train to pass that way until nearly midnight.

At five o'clock, Tim Coughlan told his men to quit for the day. A few minutes later, according to subsequent testimony, he in-

spected the burned-over area, mindful of a warning from Superintendent E. N. Armstrong to make sure that no patches were
left smoldering. Coughlan couldn't detect any traces of smoke
or flame, and at 5:30 he started homeward along the track with
his mind at ease.

Three hours later nearly everyone in Peoria, seventy-five miles
west of there, turned out to give a festive send-off to a large
crowd of local residents who were taking advantage of the
TP&W's exceptional bargain fare—$7.50—for a round trip to
Niagara Falls. The lowness of the fare was a measure of the
railroad's desperation.

"The Toledo, Peoria & Western is a bankrupt road," wrote a
Chicago newspaperman two days later. "It's one of the victims
of Jay Gould. It was a competitor of the Wabash, and in May,
1880, was leased to that road for 49½ years. In four years, Gould
and his associates had milked it dry. Then they threw it back on
the trustees of the first mortgage, where it has been ever since—
247 miles of wretched road. The corporation has been running
on nothing, and in order to lengthen out its miserable existence
has begun giving cheap excursions."

The chance to visit North America's most famous and copious
waterfall at the end of a parched summer, and for next to nothing, appealed mightily to the people of Peoria and other prairie
towns in that vicinity. They bought TP&W excursion tickets by
the hundreds, and, "as merry as schoolchildren," climbed aboard
a fifteen-car train at Peoria a little before eight o'clock on the
evening of August 10th. A throng of friends and relatives waved
them on their way.

The excursion train was made up, front to rear, of a baggage
car; a special car carrying railroad officials, some of them ac-
companied by their wives; five coaches; two Pullman chair cars;
and six sleepers. Of the TP&W's total stock of forty-eight generally debilitated locomotives, two had been found in sufficiently
good working order to pull this unusually heavy train. Even
these were not up-to-date engines, by any means. Neither was
equipped with air brakes.

Engine No. 21 was placed at the head of the train, with No.
13 coupled behind it. Engineer Edward McClintock of No. 13
had protested to the conductor, J. W. Stillwell, that the train
was too heavy and should be divided into two sections. His com-
plaint was ignored, but its validity was soon made plain by the

There was never as much of a blaze in the wreckage at Chatsworth as this Harper's Weekly artist imagined, but the rest of his scene was doubtless authentic enough, and typical of many occurring in the surrounding fields immediately after the accident. Medical help didn't arrive for nearly an hour.

difficulty the two locomotives had in stopping and starting fifteen cars, which they had to do at several stations east of Peoria in the first hours of travel. When the last contingent of excursionists had been crammed in, the train was already lagging more than an hour and a half behind schedule. At this time, Superintendent Armstrong, who was riding in the special car, counted the tickets and found there were more than six hundred persons aboard. At least one sneak thief was among them, for the journey was no more than two hours old when a passenger named Devine reported that his valise had been stolen. Perhaps with precautionary thoughts that such brethren might be in the crowd, as able to procure $7.50 to buy an excursion ticket as any honest man, several passengers had brought along revolvers. Before the night was half over, three of them used their guns for the wholly unimagined purpose of killing themselves, to escape further suffering or despair.

In midevening, heralding the approach of a change in the weather that would bring showers before dawn, a strong wind from the east began blustering across the plains around Chatsworth. A few people in town, happening to glance eastward along the railroad track around ten o'clock, were surprised to see flames flickering upward from the roadbed somewhere in the black distance. Evidently, they told themselves, the wind had fanned some sparks into fire where the grass-burners had been at work all afternoon. No one went out to try to beat down the blaze, however; it was considered insignificant and no threat to anybody's property. Open fields stretched for miles between Chatsworth and Piper City.

A grass fire had indeed been rekindled, and at about this time was crawling through the spotty patches of unburned grass close to the supports of the wooden culvert between Chatsworth and Piper City. The hay beneath the culvert had been cropped a week earlier, but it still lay there. Soon it was supplying very dry kindling for a brisk blaze that began consuming the foundations of the culvert.

The excursion train's last pickup stop was at Forest, seven miles west of Chatsworth, and with no more halts for passengers contemplated, the engineers of Nos. 21 and 13 were doing their best to make up lost time. The train covered the six miles between Forest and Chatsworth in seven minutes, and thundered through the latter town at a quarter to twelve.

The railroad excursion to Niagara Falls that ended in a heap three miles east of Chatsworth, Illinois, produced one of the most thoroughly wrecked trains in history. This rare photograph shows the splintered ruins on the morning after.

Three miles farther on, Engineer Sutherland of the leading No. 21 suddenly noticed low flames a short distance ahead. For a fraction of a second, he dismissed them as a small blaze in the grass beside the track. But as the train rushed on, he was horrified to realize that the culvert in his path was afire. Instinctively, he whistled for brakes, but at the same instant his locomotive arrived on top of the burning culvert, which crumbled beneath it. Miraculously, the leading engine cleared the gap and landed squarely on the firm track beyond, but its tender was ripped off and overturned. No. 13 dropped into the dry streambed, and nine following cars promptly "piled up as high as telegraph poles," crushed together by the heavier weight and forward momentum of the six sleepers behind them. The first sleeper came to a stop at the western edge of the burning culvert.

The high-speed derailment made instant kindling wood of the forward cars, the second coach completely telescoping the first, and the pile-up hurling Conductor Stillwell, who had been riding in the fifth coach, literally into the arms of Andy Mooney, of Peoria, who had been seated in the second. Engineer McClintock of No. 13 was killed as his engine fell into the gulley; the fireman was critically injured. Superintendent Armstrong was flung out a window of the somersaulting special car, landing painfully in a field, where he was forced almost at once to crawl out of the way of blistering steam and water blowing off from No. 13's ruptured boiler.

Engineer Sutherland hadn't even paused to assess the extent of the ruin behind him. He had sent No. 21 racing for Piper City to spread the alarm and collect medical help, which he brought back within three-quarters of an hour.

The progressive disintegration of the forward cars took up the shock of the abrupt stop to such an extent that no one in the sleeping cars was hurt seriously, and from there help first arrived.

"I was in the rear sleeper," recounted E. A. Van Zandt, of Peoria, "and so was in no danger, as no one in the six sleepers was more than shaken up. But even there we got a bad shake. I felt three distinct bumps, and then rushed out of the car and ran forward to the wreck. There the scene was horrible. The only light was the flames of the burning bridge, and above it the day coaches were piled on top of one another in a mass. The engine was buried in the ditch. . . .

"From all sides came groans and cries for aid, so we went to

A photograph guided the artist who drew the picture above of rescue and salvage activities going on simultaneously at the site of the Chatsworth wreck on the following day. The remains of cars that were heaped as high as the telegraph poles in the distance have been pulled apart and shoved off the track. The upright, relatively undamaged car was doubtless the ninth in line.

work, and we had to work hard, too. If the wreck ever caught
fire, three hundred people would have been burned to death,
and the only thing we could do was to smother the fire with
dirt."

There was no source of water within three miles or more, and
the amateur firemen had nothing to work with but their hands.
Some fifty of them clawed at the sun-baked earth until their fin-
gers bled, and for several hours fought to quench persistently re-
surgent flames with showers of dirt. They succeeded so well in
their exhausting efforts that only two cars caught fire, and they
were no more than partly charred. Rain began to fall shortly before dawn.

While other unhurt survivors from the sleeping cars started
trying to extract the injured and dead from the heap of smashed
coaches, someone carried news of the disaster to Chatsworth.
Moments later, all the fire bells and church bells in the town
were being rung, and before long the aroused townspeople were
galloping their buggies, carts, and lumber wagons over the hard
plains toward the scene of the wreck. When the loaded vehicles
cautiously returned, Chatsworth's largest public building, which
contained fire-engine stalls on the first floor and the town hall
on the second, was converted into a hospital.

In Peoria, on the following morning, the papers carried only
sketchy accounts of the wreck, with estimates of casualties that
were far below the actual figure. These were enough to alarm the
city. Troubled crowds gathered early around the telegraph office
in Thursday's scorching sunlight, which seemed to have gained in
intensity after the predawn showers. Soon a bulletin was posted
that stunned the throng with a casualty figure that came close to
the truth: at least seventy-five persons had been killed. At noon,
Peoria's normal business activities were abandoned altogether,
for at that time the mayor received a telegram from the railroad's
Superintendent Armstrong stating that one hundred and ten
bodies had been taken from the wreck. Shortly afterward, a second telegram from Armstrong raised the toll to one hundred and
twenty-five. These counts were as exaggeratedly high as the initial reports had been low. Quite understandably, as a Chicago
Tribune correspondent wrote, "they caused an absolute panic of
terror and dread." The Peoria Transcript began printing hourly
handbills containing the latest telegraphic news from the scene
of the wreck, and its staff tossed them out second-story windows

into the immense gathering in the streets. People were knocked down and trampled in the rush to grab the news.

Upon subsequent, more sober, assessment of the extent of the calamity, final totals of eighty-two killed and more than one hundred injured were arrived at. These figures confirmed as fact the already widely printed assumption that the Chatsworth disaster had at least matched Ashtabula's and was probably the worst in American railroading history to that date.

At the coroner's inquest, which began on the second floor of Chatsworth's schoolhouse the night after the wreck, Roadmaster Ennis of the TP&W voiced his conviction that the burning culvert that precipitated the wreck had been deliberately set afire by men intent on plundering the victims. (There had, indeed, been some pilfering after the wreck, but presumably it was done by fellow passengers.) Ennis revealed that three years earlier, a couple of attempts had been made to derail the 10:00 P.M. express at that same culvert by piling loose ties on the track, and that for six weeks after each discovered attempt the railroad had stationed a watchman there to guard against repeated efforts to wreck the train. "It is a very lonesome spot," Ennis remarked, "far from any house."

The railroad's president supported Ennis's view, but Superintendent Armstrong told the jurors, "I do not think it possible that anybody could have been so fiendish as to burn the bridge."

Armstrong's feeling was reinforced by a cool appraisal from J. O. Baker, a professor of civil engineering at the University of Illinois and president of the Illinois Society of Engineers. Professor Baker visited the scene of the Chatsworth disaster a day or two after it happened. He then told the press:

> The incendiary theory has no foundation whatever. I am unable personally to find any citizens of Chatsworth who have seen suspicious characters loitering about, as required by that theory. The flames of the burning culvert were plainly seen from Chatsworth at intervals for several hours before the accident. From the lay of the land, they must have risen five or six feet above the track to have been seen so far.
>
> It is plain [Professor Baker continued] that an attempt has been made to protect the bridges of the road from fire, but a personal inspection of other culverts in that vicinity shows that it was not done so as to afford complete protection. A

personal inspection along the line of the road for several miles shows that grass and weeds were not all burned off, but many patches were left unburned, and in the immediate vicinity [of the wreck] it was more carelessly done than elsewhere. The culvert itself was of the usual build and of abundant strength to carry the train, but for the fire which had destroyed the lower portion.

Professor Baker concluded that a change in the wind had stirred the embers of the afternoon's grass fires into life again after Tim Coughlan and his gang had left. Either that, he added, or sparks from Roadmaster Ennis's inspection train had fallen in unburned grass and started fresh fires.

The coroner's jury dismissed this last possibility and placed full blame for the Chatsworth wreck on Tim Coughlan, declaring that he had been "guilty of criminal carelessness in leaving fires burning near the woodwork of the trestle."

Newspaper editors tended to find this decision unfair. One wrote that it "shows the absurdity of intrusting an inquiry concerning so great a disaster to the village postmaster and four or five farmers. . . ." The jury, he continued, "appears to have desired to free the company from responsibility so far as possible, for it has not a word to say about the policy of sending so long and heavy a train over the road at a high rate of speed in the night without adequate braking appliances."

Testimony had already brought out the fact that the TP&W's Engines No. 21 and 13 were not equipped with air brakes, but when the Illinois railroad commissioners finished with their own inquiry into the causes of the Chatsworth wreck, they, too, censured Coughlan for carelessness; they said nothing about the quality of TP&W brakes or the questionable wisdom of sending out a heavily loaded fifteen-car train equipped only with hand brakes.

Fortunately, many newspapers wouldn't let the issue drop. They reminded their readers of the now-celebrated field trials of various brake systems by the Master Car-Builders Association at Burlington, Iowa, in May of that same year. These tests clearly showed the great superiority of electrically operated air brakes, which enabled a fifty-car loaded freight train to be brought to a stop from 40 mph within 450 feet.

The best air brakes of the time wouldn't have prevented a derailment at Chatsworth, for the engineer of No. 21 hadn't seen the flames of the burning culvert, he said, until he was within 300 feet of them, but they would have decisively reduced the severity of the disaster.

What was important to remember, one influential newspaper editor declared, was that "a stingy and foolish company will continue to use poor brakes until public opinion and a loss of business compel its managers to obey the dictates of common sense."

Common sense alone wouldn't do the job of protecting railroad travelers, however; a Federal law was required. Six years after the midnight catastrophe at Chatsworth, the Railroad Appliances Act of 1893 became law, and U.S. railroads thereafter were obliged to equip themselves with air brakes.

11

Washout at Dry Creek

(Eden, Colorado: August 7, 1904)

O N a rain-drenched Sunday evening, August 7, 1904, a Missouri Pacific express named *World's Fair Flyer,* on its way southward from Denver to the now nearly forgotten Louisiana Purchase Exposition at St. Louis, was broken in half by the collapse of a wooden bridge into a Colorado stream made suddenly wide, deep, and vicious by cloudbursts in the foothills of the Rockies. The train's crowded smoker and chair car, its baggage and express cars, and its 90-ton locomotive were tumbled downstream, large portions of the wreckage being swept nearly two miles below the scene of the disaster. Two partially occupied sleepers and an empty diner, at the rear end of the express, were stopped at the very edge of the break in the track by a quick-thinking porter in the leading sleeper, who intuitively set the emergency brake when he heard an outcry of terror from the cars ahead. Neither he nor anyone else in the sleepers knew what had happened until they piled off the train, which had been moving no faster than a man could walk as its engineer, Henry Hinman, warily eased the locomotive forward over the bridge, only inches above the turbulent dark waters. Abruptly, the bridge and the front half of the train had disappeared in the flood.

The accident, which happened at a place with the singularly ironic name Dry Creek, was unquestionably the worst bridge disaster that ever occurred on an American railroad. It was one of the deadliest of all U.S. railway wrecks. The Interstate Commerce Commission stated that the official toll of lives was eighty-eight, but this figure was admittedly tentative and probably low. The smoking car and chair car of the *World's Fair Flyer* had been crowded with passengers, most of whom got on the train at Colorado Springs shortly after seven o'clock that evening. An hour later, they had all drowned except one, J. M. Killen, who somehow was washed out of the smoker, kept his head above the

All that was left of the chair car of the World's Fair Flyer on the morning after the bridge washout at Dry Creek, August 7, 1904, was this barely recognizable hulk, awash in a shallow lake formed by the receding flood. This car had been crowded with excursionists.

violent current, and was tossed onto a sandy ledge, where he lay, too exhausted to move, until searchers with lanterns found him. The only other survivor from the wrecked portion of the train was Fireman Mayfield, who jumped from the cab onto firm ground at the far side of the bridge just as the engine fell backward into the water.

The *World's Fair Flyer* (MP's Train No. 11), cleared, by special arrangement, to travel over Denver & Rio Grande tracks from Denver to Pueblo, had left the Colorado capital at 5:00 P.M. on August 7th. It ran through sharp showers between there and Colorado Springs, but by the time it reached Eden, eight miles above Pueblo, the fitful rain had stopped. A mile beyond Eden, in a declivity locally known as Steele's Hollow, lay Dry Creek. The creek's name was appropriate most of the year; usually there was not a drop of water in it. Spring runoffs of melting snows, however, and periodic flash floods of other years had carved a streambed 15 feet deep and 50 feet wide through the gravelly plain, which tilted downward from the high mountains in a southeasterly direction.

At Steele's Hollow, a three-span wooden bridge, 96 feet long and 20 feet high, carried the D&RG track over Dry Creek. The bridge was only two years old, for in 1902 an earlier flash flood had washed out its predecessor. A thousand feet upstream, the creek was spanned by a less substantial wagon bridge.

Two trains had crossed Dry Creek on Sunday not long before No. 11 came along. Rain had been falling intermittently most of the day, and because some of the showers had been severe downpours, train crews and track gangs had received special orders to be on guard against washouts. Neither of the trains that preceded the doomed express had reported trouble, however, and there seems to have been no way in which Engineer Hinman could have been forewarned, except by his own discretion, not to cross Dry Creek at eight o'clock that evening. The cloudbursts that sent a wall of water plunging down the creek course, with a volume estimated at 4,000 cubic feet a second, happened within thirty minutes before the express reached Steele's Hollow.

But it was not the tremendous impact of water alone that destroyed the railroad bridge over Dry Creek. By calamitous timing, the flood carried away the wagon bridge upstream and hurled it at the trestle just as the express was crossing it. This abrupt increase in striking force knocked the piers out from un-

After the flood from the cloudburst had spent itself, a big crane was put to work grappling in deep mud for the remains of the locomotive, not visible above the streambed in this photograph. The force of the flood was greatly increased by the narrowness of the channel.

der the track, dropping the engine and forward cars of the train into the torrent.

Fireman Mayfield, though scarcely coherent when rescuers reached him, told of having stared apprehensively ahead as the locomotive crawled across the bridge. The searchlight's beam didn't reveal anything wrong with the track, he said, but it clearly showed how close the raging water was to the rails, and one wonders how Engineer Hinman dared take a chance on crossing the creek under such forbidding circumstances.

No. 11's locomotive was nosing onto solid ground again when Mayfield said he felt the bridge giving way beneath them. He yelled to Hinman to jump, but the engineer seemed paralyzed with fright. Mayfield did jump, and miraculously escaped falling into the water. The engine slumped backward and fell off to the right as it sank from sight, along with the four following cars.

The dazed passengers from the sleepers who had rushed out to see what was wrong were left staring unbelievingly into blank, roaring darkness, aware that there was nothing they could do but wait for help to arrive. Someone ran back along the track to the station at Eden, and the telegraph operator there sent the stunning news to Denver and Pueblo. Relief trains were soon on their way from both directions, but the flood subsided slowly. Even at 1:00 A.M., when Division Superintendent Bowren and a large search party arrived from Denver, the level of the stream had not dropped enough to reveal any of the sunken cars.

Pueblo's chief of police came up with twenty-five armed deputies and more than two hundred volunteer helpers. The deputies were ordered to shoot at sight anyone caught pilfering, but fortunately there were no suspected instances of it. By dawn, both banks of Dry Creek for two miles were lined with men hunting for wreck victims. Among them was Fireman Mayfield, muttering over and over again, "Poor Hinman! I must find him." When the engineer's body was finally discovered, nearly buried in sand, like many of the others, it lay more than two hundred yards below where the bridge had stood. One body was carried along by the flash flood as far as Pueblo, seven miles away.

In telegraphing his first official report on the accident to D&RG headquarters, Superintendent Bowren said, "The express car safe was open when found, but do not think robbed. Baggage and express cars broken to pieces and washed downstream, except for safe, which was recovered. Smoker and chair car also destroyed.

"I think estimate of seventy [dead] probably correct. Have no means of getting accurate figures until conductors' bodies are found and tickets counted. Brakeman who went through coaches after leaving Colorado Springs thinks this number about correct.

"Train No. 4 passed over bridge about 45 minutes before No. 11 reached there.

"The cloudburst occurred between 7:30 and 8:00, but heaviest water from hills evidently didn't reach track until after No. 4 had passed bridge."

It was wishful thinking indeed on Superintendent Bowren's part to expect to find all the tickets in the conductors' pockets when their bodies were dug out of the silt-laden passengers cars, and there was never any certain way of determining exactly how many persons died in this wreck. A passenger on one of the sleepers had spent some time in the smoker after dinner, and said he thought there were one hundred people in that car alone. Division Superintendent Bowren's estimate soon proved to be low, for eighty-eight bodies were eventually identified, but there is no telling how many more were buried forever under the quicksand of Dry Creek.

The coroner's jury that investigated this disaster found no individual to blame. It did not even question the engineer's judgment. It did, however, censure the Denver & Rio Grande for not having anticipated that the wagon bridge might someday be swept against the railroad bridge by a flash flood, and for not having strengthened it against that eventuality. In retrospect, it also felt that the railroad should have built a single-span bridge, preferably of masonry, over Dry Creek. Finally, it declared that the railroad should have had more thorough track inspection, though obviously no track inspector could have warned of a potential washout at Dry Creek unless he had been sitting on the bank for a half-hour before the *World's Fair Flyer* arrived.

In the final analysis, this formidable wreck appears to have occurred because the engineer took an unjustified risk. Had he halted No. 11 for no more than five minutes on the Eden side of Dry Creek, while he contemplated the obviously perilous situation directly ahead of the train, at least eighty-eight lives would have been saved.

12

Asleep at the Throttle
(Ivanhoe, Indiana: June 22, 1918)

THE conclusive Allied drives of the summer of 1918 had begun, and one hundred thousand American soldiers were being delivered each week to Eastern ports of embarkation from which they sailed for the battlefronts of France. The nation's overburdened railroads and their crews were showing evidences of severe strain from this massive transportation effort.

One of the many locomotive engineers involved in the continual troop movements was middle-aged Alonzo K. Sargent, of the Michigan Central Railroad, who in mid-June piloted a troop-crammed train of twenty-four new steel sleeping cars from Chicago to New York. Early on the morning of June 22nd, a clear, cool Saturday, he was driving the emptied train across northwestern Indiana on the way back to Chicago. Sargent had previously had very little sleep for more than a day, had eaten frequently in an effort to keep himself awake, and had also taken some kidney pills, which, doctors subsequently testified, contained sleep-inducing narcotics. Furthermore, the day was unusually chilly for June—thunderstorms had moved across Indiana on Friday afternoon and been followed by a cold front that brought blustering winds down from deep within Canada to cool the prairies and make the stars sparkle—and Sargent had closed his window to keep the engine cab cozily warm.

At 4:00 A.M. the vacant troop train was drumming along the rails between Gary and Hammond, about eleven miles farther west. Sargent's fireman, twenty-four-year-old Gus Klauss, a relative novice, like so many wartime railroad workers, was feeding coal into the boiler firebox and paying no attention to the engineer.

Just ahead, a few minutes earlier, the second section of a Hagenbeck-Wallace circus train, its antiquated wooden dormitory cars jauntily painted green and yellow, had attempted to switch from the Michigan Central main line to the paralleling

With wheels and axle from a cindered wooden car leaning forlornly against it, the locomotive of the Michigan Central train that struck and destroyed a Hagenbeck-Wallace circus train at about dawn on June 22, 1918, stands almost undamaged among the still-smoking ruin it caused.

track of the Gary & Western Railroad, near the tiny settlement of Ivanhoe. The Gary & Western would take the train to the fairgrounds at Hammond, where the circus was scheduled to give performances that afternoon and evening.

In the midst of the switchover, the conductor of the train sniffed the brassy stench of a hotbox and signaled the engineer to stop. The engine halted when only the first few following cars were on the Gary & Western track and the rest, some of them containing the sleeping personnel of the show, still stood on the main westbound track of the Michigan Central. The train was made up of four stock cars, carrying draft and performing horses; fourteen flatcars, bearing circus wagons and paraphernalia; four sleeping cars; and a caboose. The aged sleepers carried three hundred acrobats, aerialists, strongmen, clowns, ballet girls, animal trainers, and roustabouts, slumbering in three-tiered bunks draped with spangled costumes and drab work clothes. The cars were lighted by gas.

As the cars creaked to a stop, a flagman, carrying a lighted red lantern and some unlighted signal flares, walked eastward up the track until he stood about 600 feet behind the stalled train.

Dawn was faintly lighting the eastern sky when the flagman saw the troop train's headlight flare into view in the far distance and grow steadily brighter. The Ivanhoe towerman, Hamilton Forbes, saw it too, but watched it approach without apprehension at first, for he knew that two block signals were set against it—one cautionary, one requiring a stop—because of the presence of the circus train ahead of it on the same track. Forbes casually waited for the oncoming train, which he later said was "traveling very fast," to slow down. To his swift alarm, it did not do so. The flagman, his flares now burning fiercely and planted in the roadbed beside both rails of the track, frantically waved his lantern at the oncoming headlight. Still the troop train plunged on. As its heavy engine roared past him, the fireman desperately hurled one of the lighted flares after it. The flare landed sputtering on the floor of the cab. This was Fireman Klauss's startling first intimation that anything was wrong. He sprang up from his crouching position in front of the open firebox door and looked blearily ahead, his eyes half-blinded from the glare of the furnace. Still somewhat hazily he saw the rear marker lights of the stalled caboose directly aread. Instantly realizing that a collision was unavoidable, he leaped for the tender, where he threw himself

This view was taken from the opposite side of the locomotive. Though the rear cars of the circus train were split and hurled to both sides by the striking locomotive, most of the wreckage piled up on the right. The burned-out frame in the foreground belonged to the caboose.

face down in a pile of coal.

"That is the last thing I remember," he told questioners a few hours later. "My mind was a blank for a long time."

Meanwhile, the engineer, who had been asleep for at least the last mile and a half and probably longer, awoke to the nightmarish vision of what he thought was the tail end of a freight train only a few feet beyond the nose of his fast-moving engine. He instinctively applied the emergency brakes, but the crash came almost at the same instant—a clap of sound that awakened all of Ivanhoe.

"I was startled by a second crash," Sargent told reporters that night, "and then a third and fourth crash, as my big engine ripped through coach after coach of the train ahead. I clung to my post, and then it was all over. I got down from the cab and looked over the scene." What he saw soon made him actively sick and sent him stumbling away in shock and panic.

Witnesses who were able to crawl out of the smashed circus cars said that the fireman, too, had emerged from the upright, still largely unscathed, engine of the troop train, shouting hysterically, "He was asleep! The engineer was asleep!" He had then run yelling into some nearby woods.

No one tried to follow him. The wreck itself claimed the anguished attention of every living person in the vicinity. The last five cars of the circus train had been burst apart and crushed into splinters and tangled steel. They were strewn along the flanking ditches for several hundred feet, and the track was uprooted for the same distance. In an anachronistic re-enactment of many a train wreck of the previous century, shattered gaslights promptly set the heaped kindling ablaze, and the flames were fed by exploding gas tanks and spread by the strong north wind.

"I was asleep in the first of the four coaches, next to the flatcars in the train," said Leon Moore, a clown who became one of the heroes of the rescue efforts. "The crash awakened me. I realized the car was being telescoped. I grabbed a pillow and held it over my face. I felt myself being drawn up into a knot. When I came to myself, I felt the body of a naked person over me—a corpse.

"Someone was breaking glass," he continued, "and it fell on me. Finally, after what seemed hours, I saw the face of Emil Swire above me. One by one, people over me were removed, and finally Swire grabbed my hand. It seemed impossible for him to get me out, as I was almost helplessly pinned down.

"Then I heard an awful cry, 'The fire's coming!', and felt the stifling heat, and I believe I lost my mind. But that brave pal, Emil Swire, stuck with me, although the flames were hot about him, and I was saved."

The two men then worked as a team in the chaotic crowd of rescuers, many of them men and women in night clothes and bare feet, trying frenziedly to find missing wives, husbands, or children, for quite a few performers had their families with them. In several instances, the families, too, were part of the show.

Residents of Ivanhoe who had been shocked awake by the thunderclap of collision had immediately telephoned for help to Gary, Hammond, and even Chicago, though some of the more timid householders, fearing that wild animals had escaped from the wreck, opened their doors most furtively to survivors seeking aid and shelter, and slammed and bolted them once the strangers had been admitted. But there had been no dangerous animals aboard the stricken train. The circus menagerie had traveled on the first section of the train, which had already arrived at the Hammond fairgrounds by the time the second met disaster.

Among the first relief forces to reach the wreck was the Gary Fire Department, which found that there was no useful source of water anywhere near the blazing ruin. Until some street-sprinkling tank wagons were rounded up, firemen could do nothing but help extract the injured and carry them to where they could receive medical attention.

Newspaper photographs taken shortly after daylight showed an almost indecently intact troop-train engine standing in a smoking bed of scrap metal. Somewhere in the ruins, declared Mrs. W. F. Murphy, wife of the circus's chief canvasman, lay a fortune in jewelry and coin, though doubtless banknotes that had been in passengers' possession had long since burned to cinders. Mrs. Murphy said that she herself had lost $25,000 worth of diamonds, which she had been carrying in a chamois bag in her berth. Another woman member of the circus, Mrs. Theresa Jay, of Chicago, explained why so many valuables had been aboard. "Circus folk," she said, "are superstitious and greatly fear banks. Except for buying Liberty Bonds, they prefer to invest in diamonds or carry the money. For this reason, most of the performers had their life savings with them when the wreck occurred."

At Hammond's fairgrounds that afternoon a large crowd gathered in the faint hope that perhaps, despite the great tragedy, tradition would somehow see to it that the show went on as usual. Instead, the potential audience watched a pathetic straggle of bandaged and limping survivors report to Charles Dollmer, manager of the circus, that they were alive. A clown with a bloodied bandage around his head leaned against a tentpost and said to those within earshot, "There'll be no circus in Hammond tonight. The kids will get left this time." Then he slid to the ground in a faint.

By this time, it was known that at least sixty members of the circus company had perished in the wreck. That remained the official fatality estimate, though no one was ever sure how many roustabouts, a nomadic, carelessly identified tribe, had been killed. One hundred and twenty-five other persons on the payroll had been treated in various hospitals within a few miles of the accident. It was the worst railroad disaster that any circus in the nation had experienced up to that time, though, by a melancholy quirk of chance, this same circus had been nearly wiped out in a previous wreck, at Durand, Michigan, twenty years earlier. Already, however, the loyal fraternity of circus folk was rallying to the aid of the desolated troupe. Substitute equestriennes, animal-tamers, high-wire performers, and others were on their way to Hammond, Indiana, from all directions. By Sunday, the Hagenbeck-Wallace show rumbled out of town for its next scheduled engagement, at Beloit, Wisconsin.

On the following Wednesday, fifty-three of the victims of the wreck—only three of them identifiable—were buried in a mass grave at Woodlawn Cemetery, Chicago, after a huge public funeral. The Showman's League of America had provided the lot and would erect a tall marble memorial over the grave. Among the floral tributes was half a vanload of blossoms from the celebrated Broadway actor George M. Cohan, as well as a single rose, bearing a card that read, "From a little girl who laughed at your show and who now cries for you."

On the day after the wreck, Charles C. McChord, of the Interstate Commerce Commission, announced that ICC agents had been sent to Indiana to investigate the circumstances of the accident. He made a weak statement, though, reflecting the still inadequately muscled regulatory power of the commission, in regard to the wooden cars in which so many had died.

"We do everything we can to discourage the use of such cars on railroads and to urge the substitution of steel cars," McChord said. "We have recommended and urged that the use of wooden cars between or in front of steel cars be prohibited. That is all we can do. We shall make a thorough inquiry, however, and the public shall know all the facts."

The facts were not long in coming out, for a coroner's inquest began on Monday, June 24th. The engineer and fireman of the troop train were both present. After leaving the scene of the wreck right after it happened, Engineer Sargent had found his way to the South Shore Electric line. Here he re-encountered Fireman Klauss, who had recovered from his fit of hysteria and come out of the woods intent upon seeking the solace of his wife and children in Michigan City, Indiana. Sargent rode there with him on the electric cars, and rested for a time before proceeding to his own home in Kalamazoo, Michigan. Police arrested him when he got there. Klauss, too, was taken into custody.

At the inquest, the conductor of the troop train testified that immediately after the crash he had found Sargent staring dazedly at the flaming wreckage and had said to him, in a notable example of understatement, "This is quite a mess. How did it happen?" Sargent, he related, had replied, "I was dozing—I must have been dozing," and had then walked away, like a man in a trance.

Sargent, in his turn, revealed that he had been fighting to keep awake for some time before the collision, that he had eaten more than usual in an effort to combat his drowsiness, and that he had taken kidney pills for a nagging ailment. ["His condition was the result of some illness," said his lawyer, provided by the Michigan Central, "and was unavoidable."] Doctors testified that the kidney pills would make anyone sleepy. It was evident, and Sargent's attorney openly declared, that the engineer had indeed been unconscious when his engine passed the warning signals a mile and a quarter east of the scene of the wreck, for he had no recollection of seeing them.

The towerman at Ivanhoe, a quarter-mile east of the collision site, testified that Sargent's train had not slowed a fraction as it passed the first tower, nor had it when it passed his own, whose signals were commanding the engineer to stop. The troop train was moving so fast, declared the Ivanhoe towerman, that if it hadn't hit the circus cars, it would have been derailed automatically for running through the red lights at the Ivanhoe tower; the engineer, he said, couldn't possibly have stopped in time to avoid derailment.

Fireman Klauss, when called to the stand, explained that it was not his duty to watch for signals except when he had nothing more urgent to do, and just before the accident he was attending to a task of higher urgency—shoveling coal into the boiler furnace to keep the steam pressure up.

The coroner's verdict, reached with obvious reluctance [there was no jury], was like most others of its kind in railroad history: The train crew was found not guilty of criminal negligence; circumstances were extenuating. He doubtless felt, as other coroners, judges, and juries have felt, that clear-cut individual responsibility for a train wreck is almost impossible to demonstrate; that there are inevitably degrees to which other individuals, to say nothing of the railroad company itself, share in the blame. Rather than risk placing an unjust burden of punishment on one person, these various dispensers of judgment have chosen to let the accused go free to lose their jobs and suffer tortures of conscience far more punishing than anything the law could devise.

Only once, so far as can be determined, has the trial of a railroad engineer after a wreck resulted in a conviction and jail sentence. That was in 1942, when the engineer of a Baltimore & Ohio express that plowed into another, which was stalled, was found guilty of manslaughter and sentenced to prison for two and a half years. Railroad labor leaders declared that they were astonished at this outcome and could remember nothing like it before.

13

A Terrible Week in the War

(Wayland, New York: August 30, 1943 — Frankford Junction, Pennsylvania: September 6, 1943 — Canastota, New York: September 7, 1943)

IN the course of seven and a half memorable days in the late summer of 1943, when the nation was nearing the peak of the greatest war effort in its history, wrecks of three renowned express trains in quick succession aroused wide suspicion that enemy saboteurs were out in force to destroy the U.S. railway system, or that the system was beginning to break down.

Within scarcely more than a week, the *Lackawanna Limited,* the *Congressional Limited,* and the *Twentieth Century Limited* were all violently derailed. One hundred and twelve persons died as a result of the three accidents; two hundred and seventy-four others were injured in them. In the *Congressional Limited's* smashup alone, nearly half as many passengers were killed as had died in all U.S. railway accidents throughout the entire decade of the 1930's.

World War II placed massive burdens on American railroads. Passenger traffic in 1942 rose 82 percent above that of 1941, and in 1943 climbed 60 percent higher still. Freight traffic during the same period increased 34 percent in 1942 and 30 percent more in 1943. To cope with these extraordinary strains on the basic national heavy-transportation system, the railroads were obliged to draft aging and previously retired rolling stock into service and operate crowded schedules with too few trained personnel and "many green hands," as Joseph B. Eastman, director of the Office of Defense Transportation, described them. Maintenance was often slipshod, carelessness increased. Railroadmen were overworked and overtired much of the time; equipment was overworked and sometimes gave out.

Inevitably, railroad accidents increased, too, by more than 50 percent in the first six months of 1942 alone. Still, when critics pointed out that one hundred and seventy-five people had been killed in seven major train wrecks between 1940 and 1943, they were sharply, and justly, reminded that in the single year of 1941 more than forty thousand Americans had died in automobile accidents. It was obvious to those who took the trouble to examine comparative statistics that railroad travel was still far and away the safest form of mass transportation. Only, that was hard to remember when a bad train wreck caught and held the public's horrified attention.

The railroad tragedies of the particularly fateful period of August 30–September 7, 1943, began with a sideswiping collision on Monday afternoon between the *Lackawanna Limited,* racing along at 70 mph to make up twenty minutes' lost time, and a freight engine that blunderingly stuck its nose out of a siding into the path of the express. The accident occurred at 5:25 P.M. in the small western New York community of Wayland. Both locomotives involved were powered by steam.

More than five hundred passengers were aboard the eleven-car express, including several members of the Women's Land Army, on their way to help harvest crops upstate. These young women were riding in a coach belonging to the Nickel Plate Railroad. Their car was to be switched to that line at Buffalo.

A freight siding paralleled the main tracks of the Delaware, Lackawanna & Western at Wayland, and a switch engine had been busy there for some time before the express came along. The switcher's veteran engineer, A. T. Driscoll, later explained that the *Lackawanna Limited* arrived at the spot sooner than he had expected. He hadn't completed the afternoon's switching job, and thought he had time to finish it before the express showed up. For this reason, he was moving the switch engine along the siding when the *Limited* came thundering up from behind, having already made up ten of its lost twenty minutes between its last station and Wayland, where it was not scheduled to stop.

The switch leading into the siding was closed. An automatic wayside signal 1,500 feet east of the switch on the main line properly indicated to the engineer of the express that the track was clear. A matching light inside his cab confirmed the trackside signal. James E. Leroy, driving the *Limited* that afternoon, saw the switcher ambling along the siding in the same direction he was traveling, but naturally assumed it would stop before it got to the switch. When he realized the shocking fact that it was

In the glare of searchlights on the evening of Labor Day 1943, Pennsylvania Railroad cranes are shown at work prying apart the smashed cars of the Congressional Limited, derailed at 58 mph near Frankford Junction. The signal bridge struck by flying cars is slumped over the wreckage.

RALPH MORSE, *Life* MAGAZINE © TIME, INC.

not going to stop as soon as it should, Leroy hit the emergency brake, but it was too late. The pilot of the switch engine already protruded across the track of the express. The *Limited*'s locomotive sliced off the front end of the switcher and split its boiler, derailing itself and several following cars, and stumbling 300 feet beyond the switch before falling on its right side.

The savage jolt shattered nearly every window in the express, sending a blizzard of broken glass flying through the cars. Live steam and scalding water burst from the broken boiler of the switch engine and flooded the windowless Nickel Plate coach, which had shaken to a stop directly beside it. Twenty-six passengers in that car, including some of the Women's Land Army recruits, were almost instantly killed by the searing vapors and scalding deluge. The twenty-seventh victim of this strange wreck was the DL&W's superintendent of locomotives, F. H. Meincke, who had been riding in the cab with the engineer and fireman, both of whom were uninjured in the wreck. Meincke had jumped out of the right-hand window of the locomotive, only to have the toppling engine fall upon him. Two other passengers died of their injuries shortly after the wreck.

Wayland was too small to have a hospital, but summoned doctors and ambulances from near and far, meanwhile making its Masonic Hall, other public buildings, and several private homes available to the one hundred and fifty injured persons.

That night, though the community had had a practice blackout scheduled, potential air raids were forgotten as floodlights were hastily rigged up and automobiles angled so that their headlights would help illuminate the accident scene, a crazy sprawl of railway cars blocking all DL&W tracks. Rescuers and repair crews worked through the night.

Nearly four months later, on December 23rd, Coroner James J. Sanford, of Bath, New York, announced that his inquest had shown the wreck to have been the result of "negligence of employees and failure of officials of the Delaware, Lackawanna & Western Railroad to provide adequate safety facilities." The coroner concluded, however, that "no useful purpose would be served by recommending criminal prosecution."

Although the negligence of the freight engineer was apparent enough, it is difficult, in retrospect, to see how even the most elaborate safeguards could have prevented the fearful consequences of his sudden, last-minute wrong decision. Here, it

The wrecked and overturned locomotive of the Lackawanna Limited *lies on a bed of uprooted ties after its collision at 70 mph with a switch engine at Wayland, New York, on August 30, 1943.*

seems, is a clear case of the kind of human failure it is impossible to forestall, and from which no form of transportation, unless it be entirely automatic, can ever be immune.

On Labor Day, a week after the wreck at Wayland, almost at the same hour of the day—6:08 P.M.—a far worse accident occurred on the Pennsylvania Railroad's main line at Frankford Junction, on the northeastern edge of Philadelphia.

A moment or two earlier, three-quarters of a mile west of there, the engineer of a yard switcher was startled to see flames and smoke flaring from a journal box on one car of the New York-bound *Congressional Limited* as it flashed past him around a curve at 58 mph. He jumped to the ground and ran to tell a yard clerk, who dashed to a telephone and called the nearest tower operator to the east. The tower operator got the message just as the electric locomotive of the fast express, scheduled to make only one stop between Washington and New York, sped under his tower. He instantly telephoned the operator of the next tower, nine-tenths of a mile beyond, but before the *Congressional Limited* got that far, it fell apart, in spectacular fashion.

The blazing journal—a housing for one end of an axle—was on the front truck of the seventh car of the sixteen-car train. On the stretch of track between the two alarmed tower operators, the overheated forward axle of the seventh car suddenly broke. Instantly that car, a coach, shot almost vertically upward and turned over. In doing so, it broke its connection to the six cars ahead but yanked the following coach, two diners, and four parlor cars off the track after it. The coach that reared was sliced through from top to bottom and end to end as it struck one of the steel girders supporting a signal bridge spanning the tracks. The coach behind it slammed into the wreckage with such force that it was bent into the shape of a rough U. Passengers were flung through windows and down embankments. In the diners, a Marine captain reported, "people, tables, and food were hurled into the aisles, and a tiny child went sliding by on the floor. I tried to grab it but missed. I learned later that it was unharmed."

Live wires severed by the tumbling cars dangled over the stricken train, and one of them briefly set fire to the poleaxed first coach. The blaze was quickly extinguished. A freakish element of the accident was the fact that the vestibules at both ends of the derailed coaches were crushed shut. Rescue workers, including many members of the armed forces who were riding in the undamaged cars of the train, had to burn their way into the cars with blowtorches in order to extricate many of the dead and injured. One woman was imprisoned to her waist in a tangle of steel, and remained conscious in that dreadful situation for nearly six hours while her rescuers strove to free her. She died soon after they were able to take her to a hospital.

The death toll of this extraordinary wreck, the worst in a quarter-century, reached eighty within the week that followed. One hundred and fifteen passengers were hurt.

Only ten and a half hours after the wreck of the *Congressional Limited,* the New York Central's eastbound *Twentieth Century Limited* was derailed in an accident reminiscent of railroading a hundred years earlier. The *Century* was being hauled by a steam locomotive through quiet countryside near Canastota, in central New York State, when suddenly, at 4:34 A.M., its boiler burst. The explosion killed the engineer, fireman, and relief fireman, ripped the locomotive to shreds, and derailed ten cars of the seventeen-car train, strewing them across the entire roadbed. Only seven persons were hurt, five of them railway clerks who had been at work in the combination mail-and-baggage car when the accident occurred.

The wreck might have been far worse had it not been for the quick thinking of one of the trainmen, who, remembering that a fast freight was due momentarily from the opposite direction, ran down the tracks and flagged it to a stop before it could plow into the wrecked express.

Not one of the one hundred and seventy-three passengers aboard the *Century* was killed, despite the fact that a club car and one of the Pullmans, in which many persons were asleep, shot off the tracks into an adjoining field.

By bizarre coincidence, another locomotive, hauling an Erie passenger train at Port Jervis, in the southeastern part of New York State, blew up just a half-hour before the *Century*'s did. The Erie engineer and firemen were severely injured, and two cars were derailed, but none of the passengers on the train was hurt.

Squads of FBI agents joined ICC and other official investigators of the Pennsylvania and New York Central wrecks, because, in the wartime atmosphere, sabotage was strongly suspected. The FBI soon announced, however, that there was no evidence of foul play in either wreck. The *Lackawanna* accident had been so obviously accidental that the possibility of sabotage was not even suggested.

The blazing journal—more familiarly known as a "hotbox"— that brought the *Congressional Limited* to ruin stirred some newspaper controversy. Howard W. Starr, of Old Bennington, Vermont, writing to the editor of the New York *Times,* deplored the use of "the antiquated journal-and-box bearing" in the running gear of such a celebratedly fast passenger train as the *Congressional Limited,* when Western passenger trains of comparable speed used the much safer roller bearings in their wheels. He was promptly answered in the same medium by a defender of the Pennsy, who said that railroad had "a great many coaches equipped with roller bearings." Then why, retorted Mr. Starr, weren't they used on crack trains like the *Congressional Limited?*

The most appropriate explanation of the railway disasters of August 30–September 7, 1943, was made by Joseph B. Eastman.

"The country's railroads," he said, "are under tremendous pressure and are forced to drive their equipment as it never has been driven before."

14

Death Rides the Babylon Express

(Rockville Centre, Long Island: February 17, 1950—Richmond Hill, Long Island: November 22, 1950)

A GANTLET is a kind of braid of railroad tracks that interlaces two separate pairs of rails for a brief distance, then unravels them into independent tracks again at the end of that stretch. From where the tracks curve inward to overlap to where they curve outward to separate, four rails parallel each other on the same set of ties. The gantlet is normally for temporary use, and obviously for the use of only one train at a time.

In February 1950, the bankrupt and mishap-plagued Long Island Rail Road, carrying a daily burden of more than four hundred thousand often complaining commuters into and out of New York City, had installed a gantlet to ease the heavy two-way traffic on its Montauk branch around a grade-crossing project 1,500 feet west of the station at Rockville Centre, a community some twenty miles east of midtown Manhattan. This portion of the LIRR's 923 miles of track is electrified.

At 10:35 P.M. on the clear night of February 17th, a twelve-car express bound for Babylon, east of Rockville Centre, struck an incoming eight-car train from Babylon almost head-on at the west entrance to that gantlet. The westbound Train No. 175 for New York City had left Rockville Centre only a moment or two before and was barely under way. The eastbound train, on the other hand, had already run past a warning signal and a stop signal and had not yet slowed appreciably for an imminent scheduled halt at Rockville Centre. Its head car met the leading car of the New York-bound train just as the latter was curving out of the gantlet at 12–15 mph and the former was swinging into it at 30–35 mph. The two cars collided with a metallic din that rang through the startled neighborhood. The collision meshed the left sides of both cars, tearing them apart.

"There was a tremendous shock," reported a college student

Firemen and volunteer rescue workers search the ruins of the leading cars of two Long Island Rail Road trains that collided, almost head-on, at Rockville Centre on the evening of February 17, 1950. The cars at right sliced through the coach at left from end to end.

who had been riding in a following car of the eastbound train. "My head hit the wall, and all the lights in the train went out."

Both leading cars were well filled with passengers, for the first and last cars of Long Island trains were customarily reserved for smokers. Furthermore, the Babylon express that had left Pennsylvania Station, in New York City, at 10:03 on that Friday evening was one of the most heavily patronized evening trains of the line. It was favored by commuters who chose to go to a movie and avoid rush-hour crowds before making their homeward journeys to the Island. Some of them were now piled five deep in the crash at Rockville Centre.

The loud clang of collision and brilliant flashes of electricity from the short-circuited third rail quickly drew thousands of on-lookers to the scene. Travelers waiting in Pennsylvania Station for subsequent Long Island trains were almost the last members of the radio-alerted metropolitan public to learn what had happened. Their first hint of trouble came in ambiguous public notices that were posted near the train gates on the lower level of Penn Station: "Due to obstructions at Rockville Centre, passengers for points east of Valley Stream are subject to a one-hour delay. Bus service will be furnished between Valley Stream and Freeport, and trains will be operated from Freeport to Babylon." Frustrated commuters turned away cursing the Long Island for one more in a long, wearying series of inconveniences, and went their separate ways before finding out that the "obstructions" at Rockville Centre were entangled passenger cars in which twenty-nine persons had been killed outright and at least seventy-nine others hurt. Three of the latter soon succumbed to their injuries, raising the final death toll to thirty-two.

Within a short time after the collision, welders had been lowered to the roofs of the wrecked cars from a trestle directly above and were cutting paths through crumpled steel to enable doctors and stretcher-bearers to reach the live and dead victims. The Second Baptist Church, near the tracks, had become a field quarters for the Red Cross, police, and clergymen, and an emergency operating theater for surgeons.

Probably because the motormen of the collided trains rode at the right side of their respective cars, and thus out of the direct line of impact, neither had been seriously injured. Both were interviewed on the night of the accident by men from the office of the district attorney of Nassau County. James W. Markin, who had been driving the train that had just pulled out of Rockville Centre station for New York City when it was hit, was released after questioning. The district attorney, Frank A. Gulotta, said no charges would be made against him. Jacob Kiefer, the short, stocky motorman of the Babylon express, had been thrown from his cab in the crash and lay on the ground beside the wreckage, a large fragment of debris across his body, when railroad police found him. They took him to the superintendent of the line, who talked to him briefly in a nearby gateman's shanty and sent him home. Kiefer was in bed, at his anxious wife's insistence, when a young assistant district attorney, Henry R. Stern, Jr., arrived with

In the second disastrous wreck on the Long Island Rail Road in 1950, the leading car of the outbound Babylon express, which looks lighter-colored in this photograph because of the glare of searchlights, telescoped the rear car of a halted train at Richmond Hill on Thanksgiving eve.

a police surgeon and a stenographer a little after 3:00 A.M. to ask him how the accident happened.

District Attorney Gulotta told reporters later that Kiefer had admitted running through a stop signal 171 feet west of the point where the collision occurred. Gulotta refused to say whether the motorman, whose doctor declared he had a possible skull fracture, had given any explanation of why he had failed to obey the signal. The district attorney had placed Kiefer under house arrest and charged him with criminal negligence and second-degree manslaughter. If found guilty of these charges, Kiefer could be imprisoned for as long as fifteen years. The gray-haired, fifty-five-year-old motorman was arraigned on September 20th and released on $10,000 bail, raised by friends.

On the day after the wreck, the mayor of Rockville Centre declared in a letter to Governor Thomas E. Dewey that he was "shocked to learn that no automatic stopping devices supplementing automatic signal mechanisms" were in use on the Long Island tracks in his community.

"It is our understanding," wrote Mayor W. Harry Lister, "that such a mechanism, which is in use on other transit lines, would have automatically stopped the second train and prevented it from entering upon a track on which another train was already proceeding." Lister urged the Governor to exert all necessary pressure to have these devices, a standard safeguard throughout New York City's vast subway system, installed on the Long Island Rail Road.

At the outset of the New York State Public Service Commission's investigation of the wreck, officials of the Long Island offered to install within twenty-four hours a manual system of brake trippers, operated by three two-man shifts, at the Rockville Centre gantlet, over which, during rush hours, a train passed every six minutes. The commission accepted the offer, as "a temporary measure." The railroad's representative had said the need for the gantlet would end the following May, when the overpass at Rockville Centre would be finished.

The manual brake-tripping devices were set up beside signals 3,500 feet from the gantlet on either side. Less than a week after the wreck, the Public Service Commission required a further precaution to be taken: all LIRR trains must slow to 15 mph within 600 feet of the gantlet. The previous allowable speed in that vicinity was 30 mph.

The Nassau County grand jury's probe of the accident began a week after the wreck occurred. Meanwhile, the more than three hundred members of the Long Island Rail Road's chapter of the Brotherhood of Locomotive Engineers voted unanimously to pay Kiefer's legal expenses when he came to trial. Their chairman told a reporter: "Most of us have known and liked Kiefer for thirty years or more, and we don't want to let him down. None of us think he deliberately ran through a stop light. He must have blacked out. I asked him how it happened and he said he doesn't know."

District Attorney Gulotta released evidence from the railroad's personnel files that Kiefer had been cited for twenty-one previous violations of company rules and safety regulations. He added, however, that Kiefer's case was by no means exceptional. According to the records of three hundred and five motormen and engineers, "human failure" appeared to have been practically endemic on the Long Island Rail Road. The records covered a period from 1920 to 1944 and listed a total of 2,680 violations of regulations, more than half of which were considered threats to the safety of trains. One man had achieved the record number of thirty-six violations; only five men out of three hundred and five had none. Records for the last six years prior to the wreck at Rockville Centre were incomplete and unavailable, Gulotta said.

The first attempt to prosecute Jacob Kiefer ended in a mistrial two days after it began, in mid-June, because of the revelation that, contrary to specific instructions, representatives of the district attorney had questioned prospective jurors personally. A new trial was set for the middle of September. It was only then that the full story of what happened on the night of February 18th was brought out.

The situation moments before the crash was first depicted by the signal-block operator at Rockville Centre. Charles Zablocki, who had the duty that night, explained that he had given the "Medium clear" signal to westbound Train No. 175 as it pulled out of the station on its way to New York City. That action authorized its motorman, James W. Markin, to proceed through the gantlet at a speed no higher than 30 mph. At the same time, it automatically set two signals against Kiefer's eastbound Babylon express, Train No. 192. The signal closest to Kiefer, 4,000 feet west of the gantlet, warned him to cut his speed in half and prepare to stop at the so-called home signal, only 171 feet west of the gantlet. The home signal at this time indicated "Stop."

As Markin's train moved out of the station, lights flashing on Zablocki's control board informed him that Kiefer's approaching train had already passed the caution signal nearly a mile west. He assumed that Kiefer would halt it before it reached the home signal. There was nothing that Zablocki could do in case the train failed to stop.

Markin testified that his train's brakes had been tested at Babylon just before it left there, at 9:58 that evening. "Everything was working very good," he said.

"The night was clear," Markin recalled, as he responded to Zablocki's signal and moved his train out of Rockville Centre station at 10:34. "It wasn't raining and it wasn't snowing. My headlight was bright. I blew my whistle for the grade crossings west of the station, and I got over them all right.

"When I got to Bank Street, I looked to see if the eastbound train was waiting behind the home signal. I saw him coming right down on top of me. I'd say he was about forty feet away. I was going about twelve or fifteen miles an hour at the time.

"I blew my alarm whistle and dimmed my headlight and threw on the brake. Then we crashed."

Why hadn't Kiefer stopped in time to avoid the collision?

Because he was unconscious, his attorney suddenly revealed in a surprise statement—"blacked out" for two minutes while his train rolled downgrade out of control toward the point where it sliced into Markin's.

"After passing the Lynbrook station," Kiefer himself told the court, "I don't remember anything until I was at the bottom of the hill, a few seconds before the crash. When I came to, I saw the signal was against me. I heard my cab control whistle blowing and I saw the other train coming. I was only a couple of hundred feet west of the stop signal."

"What did you do?" his attorney asked.

"I threw my brake on Emergency. That was the quickest stop I could get. That's all I know. It happened so quick, in a few seconds."

"In my opinion," Kiefer's physician subsequently testified, "this patient suffered from a spasm of the blood vessels in the brain that resulted in unconsciousness for that period."

The defense counsel, James M. O'Connell, explained that Kiefer had been suffering from a sinus infection and high blood pressure for the previous two years, that he had had one fainting spell while off duty during that period, and that he had been treated for high blood pressure twice within the week of the accident, the second time on the day before it.

"Didn't you know the safety of twelve cars full of passengers behind you depended upon your being able to do your job on the night of February 17th?" the prosecutor demanded.

"Yes," said Kiefer.

"Yet you didn't report yourself sick. Why not?" the prosecutor continued.

"I didn't feel sick."

"As a matter of fact, you weren't sick at all, were you?" his questioner asked, in angry tones.

"Well, I didn't feel sick," Kiefer admitted.

Kiefer's prosecutor, the young assistant district attorney who had inteviewed him at three o'clock in the morning on February 18th, askcd rhetorically why thc motorman hadn't said anything then about having been unconscious. "Because that idea did not take form until later," he said with sarcasm, answering his own question.

The jury's growing sympathy for the apparently sincere and emotionally shaken motorman had, however, already become evident to courtroom observers. Kiefer's attorney made a powerful bid to capture it completely in his address to the jury at the conclusion of testimony.

"Can you say Jacob Kiefer drove down this grade intending to cause an accident with himself in the front end of the train?" he asked. "However this case comes out, there is no future for Jacob Kiefer. He was through the moment the accident happened. He started with the railroad at the age of twenty-one; now he is as dead as though he perished in that wreck."

Kiefer and his wife wept silently, and the jury filed out to consider its verdict. After seven and a half hours of deliberation, during which time it asked to have all of the motorman's testimony read to it from the record, the jury finally agreed upon a verdict. Returning to the courtroom, it announced its unanimous decision: "Not guilty as charged."

Kiefer, now sobbing, managed to gasp, "Thank you, gentlemen," and slumped into the arms of his wife.

The motorman's greatest worry was over, but the financially

ailing Long Island Rail Road, already scraping to settle the many damage suits brought against it as a consequence of the Rockville Centre wreck, was moving into ever deeper trouble. On August 6th, a young brakeman had opened the wrong switch near Huntington, on the north shore of the Island, causing a passenger train to run into a sidetracked freight. No one was killed, but forty-six passengers were hurt, four of them seriously so. Then, on the eve of Thanksgiving, at almost the peak of rush-hour traffic, the worst disaster in the history of the railroad occurred.

On the frosty night of November 22nd, at 6:26 P.M., in the Richmond Hill district of Queens County, just east of New York City, another twelve-car Babylon express, far more crowded than its ill-fated predecessor in February, plowed into the rear of a similarly packed train bound for Hempstead. The first train had left the terminal at Pennsylvania Station five minutes ahead of the second, but had stalled on its approach to the station at Kew Gardens, Long Island, when its brakes jammed. The collision happened with such force that the head car of the Babylon train partly telescoped the last car of the Hempstead train and burrowed beneath it. Seventy-nine persons died as a result of this crash, and three hundred and sixty-three others, including eleven railroad employees, were treated for injuries suffered in it.

Benjamin J. Pokorny, fifty-five years old, regarded by railroad officials as one of the best engineers of the line, had been driving the Babylon express. He was killed in the collision, his body not extricated until hours later. Thus, an explanation of why his train crashed into the one ahead of it had to be constructed from the testimony of other members of both train crews at the Interstate Commerce Commission hearings that promptly followed the accident.

The motorman of the Hempstead train, William M. Murphy, sixty-one years old, who had worked for the railroad for thirty-one years and as a fireman and engineer for twenty-three of them, said that the trip had gone smoothly enough until he was approaching the signal bridge spanning the tracks at Union Turnpike, west of Kew Gardens. "I then got an 'Approach' signal," he said. That meant he was to slow to a maximum of 30 mph. He complied as his train passed under the signal bridge. At this point, he could clearly see the block signal ahead, at Metropolitan Avenue. He noted that it was displaying the "Restricted" signal, which meant that he was to slow to 15 mph.

Although he intended only to comply with that speed limitation, it was here that his brakes began to grab, bringing the train to a complete stop just short of the Metropolitan Avenue signal. Murphy was in this predicament, for the first time in his experience, when he saw the Metropolitan Avenue signal change from "Restricted" to "Approach." He was now permitted to proceed at 30 mph, but he couldn't budge the train an inch.

"It was about a minute after this that we were hit," he said.

Bertram N. Biggam, a brakeman on the rear car of the stalled train, testified that he had unlocked the rear doors as the train came to a stop, and, in compliance with regulations, had stepped down to the tracks with his red lamp to flag a following train, in case one appeared. He saw nothing coming, he said, but he did hear the motors of his own train arc-ing, as they normally did when about to start up, so he climbed back onto the rear platform, and pulled the whistle-cord twice to notify the motorman that he was cleared to go ahead.

When the train failed to move, Biggam unlocked the doors again and started to descend to the tracks a second time for probable flagging operations. At that moment, he heard the Babylon express coming and saw its headlight bearing down upon him. Biggam jumped back onto the rear platform, frantically wagged his red lamp at the oncoming train, then jumped into the car intending to warn passengers of an imminent collision and tell them to get down on the floor. Before he could utter a word, the crash occurred, and he was knocked unconscious.

A New York City fireman, Fred C. Mergi, was sitting inside the car. He had watched Biggam go out with his lamp, return, pull the whistle-cord, and go out again.

"Then I guess we both saw the express coming down at the same moment," Mergi said. "This big white light flooded the car and we both went for the floor. I was lucky and slid down the aisle. The lights went out and glass crashed. Everybody was yelling and screaming. A chandelier came down on my head."

As the ICC commissioners reconstructed the course of events prior to the crash, they concluded that Motorman Pokorny, in the following train, had seen the signal light on the Metropolitan Avenue bridge change from "Restricted" to "Approach," for he had an unobstructed view of it for over 4,000 feet, and had then assumed that the Hempstead train had already moved out of the block he was entering. Fellow members of his crew said that their train had gone into the block slowly but had abruptly picked up speed to about 35 mph, presumably when Pokorny saw the signal change. When he discovered that the train ahead had not cleared the block but was stopped dead in his path, it was much too late to halt his own train. The collision occurred seconds later.

One naturally wonders why Pokorny couldn't have seen the red oil-lamp markers that the Long Island Rail Road carried on the rear cars of all its trains. The answer to that question will never be known for certain, but one striking revelation made two weeks earlier in an LIRR report to the Public Service Commission provides a clue to what the reason probably was. The Long Island Rail Road reported on December 6th, in compliance with a PSC request, that in the course of the seven preceding days, at least one red marker-light had failed on three hundred and six of its trains, while both lights had gone out on fifty trains.

It is very possible that Pokorny's first warning that Murphy's train was stalled in his path came when he saw Biggam frantically waving his red lantern from the rear platform in a last-second attempt to flag the following train to a stop.

To a metropolis whose Thanksgiving spirit was already severely dampened by the effects of the Korean War, this railroad catastrophe came as a dismaying shock, shared by millions. Rarely, commentators agreed, had so many been saddened and frightened by an accident that affected so relatively few of them directly. Partly for this reason, and partly because of the alarming frequency with which major accidents had been taking place on the Long Island Rail Road in 1950, state and local political figures now made strong, frequent statements about the imperative need to improve the safety of what Mayor Impellitteri of New York City called "this disgraceful common carrier."

Several bills had been submitted to the state legislature after the wreck of the earlier Babylon express at Rockville Centre that would have required the Long Island and all other railroads in New York State to install automatic tripping devices that would brake trains to a halt if they rode through a stop signal. All failed to pass. Most legislators were aware that only the Interstate Commerce Commission has authority to order railroads to install safety devices.

In a rather indignant commentary on these proceedings, a spokesman for the Long Island declared that automatic trippers were fine for trains that ran underground, but not for open-air railroads, especially in the Northeast, where snow and ice could interfere with the efficiency of them in winter. The Long Island had installed trippers on a few trains years before, he said, but in 1932 had petitioned the ICC to allow it to dispense with them, on the grounds that the trippers had occasionally responded when they shouldn't have and had been an expensive nuisance to maintain. The LIRR was only one of several railroads, its spokesman added, that asked the ICC to allow them to remove tripping devices after trying them out. (The ICC had granted the requests, and in 1950 admitted that it still wasn't entirely convinced of the value of trippers on all-weather railroads; that, in fact, they were in use on less than 10 percent of the nation's 230,000-mile railway network.)

After the wreck of the second Babylon express, however, the Interstate Commerce Commission within a month ordered specific modern safety systems installed on a total of fifty-three miles of Long Island Rail Road tracks.

The LIRR was told to extend the automatic cab-signal system in use on nearly all its other electrified tracks to the nine-mile section lying between Hillside, in Queens County, and the east entrance to the East River tunnel between Long Island and Manhattan Island. It was in this section that the Thanksgiving Eve disaster took place. (The system to be installed was one that causes trackside signals to be duplicated by lights in the cabs of locomotives and in motormen's compartments, and is in very common use on U.S. railroads.)

On that same portion of the line, and on some forty-four miles of tracks on other branches as well, the ICC ordered the Long Island to install a then-new automatic train-control system. This system, operating in conjunction with cab signals, would prevent any train from entering at more than 12 mph a block of track already occupied by another train.

In "recommending" these safety measures (with the proviso that court action would be taken to enforce compliance if the railroad didn't voluntarily accept them within thirty days), the ICC declared that if automatic train controls had been in use at Rockville Centre and at Richmond Hill, neither Babylon express would have caused a wreck.

15

"The Broker" Comes to a Bad End

(Woodbridge, New Jersey: February 6, 1951)

A S the gloomy afternoon of February 6, 1951, darkened into
night, Mrs. Elizabeth Szeles, who lived in a two-story frame
house facing a railroad embankment in the town of Woodbridge,
New Jersey, had the most frightening experience of her sixty-two
years.

A damp, chill evening had closed in, under a moonless and
cloudy sky. Streets wet with melt from a thinning cover of dirty
snow looked like black rivers in the glow of lights, blurred by
wraiths of ground fog.

Shortly after five-thirty, as Mrs. Szeles busied herself in her
kitchen, she was distantly aware of the rumble of an approaching
train. This was a cozily familiar sound, the daily accompaniment
to half her life.

What followed a moment later was in terrifying contrast. Outside, a prolonged, clangorous crash of tremendous volume suddenly made the ground shudder. "It shook the house like jelly,"
Mrs. Szeles told a reporter the next day. "I thought it was an
earthquake."

She ran to a parlor window and looked out into seething
clouds of smoke and steam. As she stood there, staring through
a swirl of vapors, she began to see details of a scene of horror and
wild confusion. Ripped and crumpled passenger cars, their windows shattered, their steel sides twisted, lay sprawled along the
steep slope of the muddy embankment that paralleled Fulton
Street, on which she lived. The embankment ran within a hundred feet of the Szeles residence.

In a stunned way, Mrs. Szeles became aware that inside the
crazily strewn cars there were people screaming and shouting.
She then saw some bedraggled figures stumbling across the street
toward her front door.

During the next few hours, Mrs. Szeles's tidy rooms, like those
of many other houses in the neighborhood, became first-aid sta-

Rescue workers begin the grueling job of extricating dead and injured passengers from one of the overturned coaches of The Broker *after its derailment at Woodbridge, New Jersey, on February 6, 1951.*

tions. Medical and fire-department rescue teams from a score of northern New Jersey communities rushed into the area to extricate and treat or carry off to morgues and hospitals the appallingly numerous victims of one of the worst train wrecks in the history of railroading. The accident had injured three hundred and fifty persons and had caused the deaths of eighty-four others, most of them instantly.

The precise moment of the calamity was 5:43 P.M. It had happened at a short, temporary trestle, opened to rail traffic only a little more than four hours earlier. The trestle had been built to carry the tracks of a Pennsylvania Railroad spur line across highway construction work a quarter of a mile south of the Woodbridge station. Six trains had crossed it safely before the seventh was wrecked there. The trestle was as long as a standard passenger car. The temporary track curved sharply away from the main line to span it, then swung back to the main line in a curve equally sharp.

A general order to all PRR train crews to slow to 25 mph before crossing that trestle had been issued and distributed on January 29th, eight days before the wreck. The order was to take effect at 1:01 P.M. on February 6th, the day the trestle opened to traffic. No caution flags or signal lights had been set up along the approaches, however. Kenneth J. Silvey, a PRR division engineer in charge of maintenance of way and signals, testified later that when the company issued a general "Slow" order, that obviated any requirement for signals to mark the section of track to which the order pertained.

In the immediate aftermath of the disaster, it was thought that the trestle had collapsed, and that its failure had caused the accident. More thorough investigation proved that this was not true. The trestle was indeed damaged by the derailment, but had not been the cause of it.

An hour before the wreck, the usual late-afternoon crowds of commuters and shoppers from New York City had begun streaming out of the subway that runs beneath the Hudson River into Jersey City's railroad terminal. Those homeward bound for a dozen towns and cities to the southeast, bordering the Atlantic coast, hurried through the terminal this evening with a special sense of urgency and singleness of direction. Many of them customarily caught a New Jersey Central train, but that railroad was still shut down by a national strike of switchmen, though

On the morning after the wreck of The Broker, big railroad cranes are shown at the task of clearing away the remains of the smashed train. The coach in left foreground was crumpled like a tin can.

the strike was waning. Tonight, nearly everybody headed for *The Broker*, an eleven-car Pennsylvania Railroad train scheduled to depart a few minutes past five o'clock for its daily run between Jersey City and Bay Head Junction. There was a common awareness in the hastening throng that seats on *The Broker* would be hard to find, if obtainable at all.

By departure time, the train was jammed with more than a thousand passengers, many of them obliged to stand in the aisles, maneuvering their coats and bundles and briefcases as best they could. Only the last car preserved an air of comfort and relaxation. It was a club car rented for daily use on *The Broker* by a group of commuting executives.

When, at 5:10, *The Broker* moved out of the Jersey City terminal, its regular train crew was in charge. The engineer was Joseph H. Fitzsimmons, fifty-seven years old, an employee with a long, respectable service record. He was at the throttle of a steam locomotive, one of the few still in regular service anywhere in the United States in 1951. This one, subsequent court testimony revealed, had no speedometer. Fitzsimmons's fireman was A. M. Dunn, who was to die of critical injuries less than three hours later. The conductor of the train was John H. Bishop, who had worked thirty-four years for the Pennsy. For the past five years, he had patiently borne the nickname Honest John, given him for having turned in a lost bag containing $25,000 in cash and jewels that he had found in Pennsylvania Station in 1946.

According to Bishop, before *The Broker* pulled out of Jersey City on February 6th, he and the engineer had discussed the "Slow" order pertaining to the temporary trestle at Woodbridge. There was no question, Bishop declared, but that Fitzsimmons knew about it. As the train rolled on through the lowering night, however, the conductor said he had found it difficult to tell exactly where they were at any time, except at station stops, because the aisles were so crowded and the windows so fogged by steam. He knew from long experience, though, when the train was due to be approaching Woodbridge. As that time neared, he became convinced that Fitzsimmons was driving the train much too fast for the abnormal track condition that existed beyond the Woodbridge station. Bishop felt so apprehensive that he was pushing his way through the crowd toward the nearest emergency-signal cord, to warn the engineer to slow down, when the train lurched dizzily and began to split apart.

The locomotive, tender, and first eight cars were derailed as they swung around the new, 5-degree curve leading onto the trestle. The forward portion of the train, up to the sixth car, nevertheless managed to lurch across the small bridge structure before spread-eagling over the roadbed. The engine fell on one side, tossing Fitzsimmons out of his cab and tearing up roadbed and track, but remained on top of the 26-foot embankment. The tender, laden with 20,000 pounds of coal and 10,000 gallons of water, plunged down the slope to Fulton Street, dragging the first and second cars after it. They lost their undercarriages, jackknifed, and tilted precariously, but did not turn over. The third and fourth cars plowed farther down the embankment and were massively damaged; one was bent nearly U-shaped. The fifth car flopped on one side. The sixth evidently got snagged in the trestle, dropping a pair of wheel trucks into the street beneath, and whiplashed the seventh and eighth past it. These last tore open their sides on a huge, jagged triangle of concrete that had been dislodged from the trestle abutment, and landed in a heap beside the third and fourth cars. The three remaining cars of the train stayed on the track, their occupants badly shaken and bruised but, for the most part, not seriously hurt.

In the terrible seconds of this chaotic pile-up, rows of passengers standing in the aisles were slammed against the walls like waves crashing on a beach. Rescuers later found bodies jammed into baggage racks, wedged between collapsed seats. One of them said, "The place looked like a slaughterhouse blown to hell." An injured woman's long hair was so entangled in mashed steel that it had to be cut off with a knife to free her. A man who had been hurled from a careening car lay pinned in mud under a stray wheel, moaning, "Help me! Help me!"

Numerous passengers were so shocked by their experiences that they didn't know where they were, and mistook dully glistening Fulton Street for a river, into which some of them dived to escape. Those able to talk rationally told how flying packages, briefcases, bags, seat cushions, and swordlike splinters of glass had cascaded upon the passengers as the cars tumbled and slid.

As soon as the wreck lost its savage momentum, many inside the cars who were still alive and able to move fought and kicked, punched and screamed, in a frantic scramble to escape. "They were like a bunch of wild animals trying to get out of turned-over cages," an eyewitness reported. Among them, as in all mass disasters, a few remained steady and performed feats of exceptional self-sacrifice and heroism. Most passengers who were lucky enough to emerge from the wreck unharmed and clearheaded fanned out into nearby streets, attempting to hitch rides home as soon as possible.

News of the wreck was broadcast by New York City radio stations within a few minutes, drawing to the scene not only rescue forces but swarms of anxious relatives of persons assumed to be on the train, and far greater throngs of the merely curious. Floodlights soon illuminated the wreckage, their blue-white radiance flawed at a dozen points by the sputtering yellowish flames of oxyacetylene torches, cutting tangled steel away from trapped victims, alive or dead.

Bystanders rapidly became so numerous that they got in the way of rescue workers and blocked the flow of a two-block-long procession of ambulances and commandeered trucks, lined up to transport the injured and dead. Soldiers from nearby Camp Kilmer were called in to help police control the crowds. The troops soon cleared Fulton Street of all onlookers by walking slowly down it with fixed bayonets, in street-wide rows.

Engineer Fitzsimmons, who had been thrown from the engine as it fell sideways, had relatively minor injuries: scalp cuts and fractured ribs. He now lay in a hospital bed in the Perth Amboy Hospital. In the same hospital, Fireman Dunn died at 7:20 that night.

Fitzsimmons told investigators who came to question him there, "I entered the trestle at about 25 mph, and the speed of the train certainly couldn't be blamed for the crash." His fireman's testimony on that crucial point was no longer obtainable.

A Pennsylvania Railroad detective who had been riding on *The Broker* at the time of the wreck told reporters that the train was "traveling at top speed" just before it left the track. Passengers who were questioned about the matter set the speed at from 45 to 60 mph, most of them favoring a range between 50 and 60.

On the day following the accident, a day of gusty rain that drove sightseers away and hampered repair crews in their efforts to restore normal service on the line, *The Broker*'s gaunt, unshaven engineer seemed to lose confidence in his initial statements. He admitted to New Jersey's Deputy Attorney General, Benjamin Van Tine, that the train *might* have been traveling

50 mph, twice as fast as the "Slow" order permitted, when it curved onto the temporary track to cross the Woodbridge trestle. But "all the time I was looking for a yellow light, a yellow light, a yellow light," Fitzsimmons reiterated, in a breaking voice. Then, he continued, "all of a sudden the engine seemed to slip out from beneath me. It seemed to be pulling me."

The engineer further admitted that despite the fact that he had been instinctively peering through the thin fog and darkness in search of a "Caution" light, because of his early training and experience on another railroad, he was well aware that it was not the Pennsy's practice to provide one at a section of temporary track after a "Slow" order pertaining to it had been issued.

"They do not put up lights," Fitzsimmons said, as if reciting something he had memorized. "They notify you by general order."

Both supervisory and operating personnel of the railroad confirmed this in the course of investigations conducted by the Interstate Commerce Commission and the New Jersey Public Utilities Commission.

As a result of his own inquiry into the causes of the wreck, Alex Eber, assistant prosecutor for New Jersey's Middlesex County, in which the disaster occurred, made an attack on the Pennsylvania Railroad.

"The failure to have caution signals and signs along the right-of-way at appropriate distances from existing danger points represents a complete and indifferent disregard for human life and is to be condemned," Eber said in a public statement on February 8th.

"The accepted standard and safe practice for railroad operation," he pointed out, "dictates the employment of a signal four thousand feet in advance of a point at which a train is to reduce speed, and a second signal at the restricted point."

Eber's accusatory attitude was echoed in a New York *Times* editorial the following day, which said, in part:

> Could not the railroad, which issued an admonitory bulletin more than a week in advance of the accident, have installed caution signals? Why didn't it do this? Who is to blame for its not being done?
>
> If there was a human failure, those involved in it should

certainly be removed from positions in which their neglect or carelessness can cause danger in the future. But what rapid transit really requires . . . is systems and devices that are proof against human failure.

Similar conclusions had been reached on similar occasions a hundred times before.

As if prompted by these voices of criticism, though insisting that its plans had been laid long before the Woodbridge wreck, the Pennsylvania Railroad announced three weeks later that it was going to install a $12,000,000 automatic speed-control system for trains on all its major passenger lines, including those carrying commuters to and from New York City.

The new system, declared James M. Symes, Pennsy vice-president in charge of operations, would virtually eliminate man-failure as a cause of accidents on PRR lines transporting 75,000,-000 people a year—the heaviest passenger traffic on any U.S. railroad.

Announcing the findings of its investigation of the wreck at Woodbridge, the Interstate Commerce Commission on April 19th declared that the accident, "which resulted in 84 deaths and injuries to 345 passengers and five railroad employees, was caused by excessive speed on a curve of a temporary track." The commission recommended, rather belatedly, that the Pennsylvania Railroad adopt the automatic train-control system that it had announced a month earlier it was going to install. Work on the system was already under way by then.

16

A Mysterious Plunge into Newark Bay
(Bayonne, New Jersey: September 15, 1958)

CAPTAIN Peder Pederson was appalled at what he saw materializing in the soft morning sunlight.

The big railroad lift-bridge south of his dredger, *Sand Captain*, had just been raised to allow the two-hundred-foot vessel to leave Newark Bay for a day's work of scooping sand from the ocean floor off Ambrose Lightship. Yet Pederson, staring upward incredulously from the deckhouse, could see a passenger train rapidly approaching the open bridge from the west. The five-car train, headed by two diesel locomotives, was moving at such speed that its engineer evidently was not aware of the great gap in his path.

In a frantic effort to warn the passenger train of the peril ahead, Pederson sounded his boat's distress signal. As *Sand Captain's* whistle began shrieking alarm, Pederson ordered his engine room to reverse engines at full speed. If the train were about to plunge into the ship channel, as now seemed inevitable, Pederson was not going to let his boat be caught beneath it as it fell.

He had acted just in time. The train's diesels and first three coaches, rumbling blindly forward, lunged with a roar over the edge and curved nightmarishly into deep, murky water, 40 feet below. The sound, said a seafaring man who heard it from across the channel, was like that of a big anchor-chain being dropped. The locomotives and the two forward coaches sank in a giant geyser of splashes. The third coach hung head down from the torn end of track at an angle of 80 degrees, its front buried in the swift tidal current. The two remaining coaches had shaken to an abrupt stop at the brink.

The shrill hoots of the dredger's whistle were at once joined by wails from the bridge lift-house, as its emergency siren began howling.

It was ten o'clock on the warm, hazy morning of Monday, September 15, 1958. One of the most mystifying of recent major U.S. train wrecks had run its brief, tragic course. Forty-eight persons had been killed, twenty injured.

No observer near the scene was more shocked by the accident than young Tom Sellers, who had been sitting with a friend in a rowboat only a few yards from the bridge, the two boys tending their fishlines. Tom, who was fifteen, grabbed the oars and rowed as hard as he could through crash-spawned waves toward the passenger car that still nosed downward into the roiled channel.

A gasping woman surfaced near by. Tom flung the oars to his friend and hauled her aboard. Spying a man struggling in the water, Tom then dived for him. He missed the man, injured himself somehow, lost sight of his boat when he surfaced, and finally made his way to the track level by climbing over pilings and up a steel ladder.

At the moment of 10:00 A.M., Edward McCarthy, co-owner of a small-boat anchorage a quarter of a mile northeast of the lift-bridge, was busy checking out supplies to early customers. When the mingled clamor of *Sand Captain*'s whistle and the bridge siren arose, McCarthy and a truck driver who had been unloading beer at the marina jumped into McCarthy's powerboat and sent it leaping toward the scene. As they swung alongside the partly submerged car, they could hear people screaming for help and found the water already reddening. But there was little time to note details. They, and men in a boat that had put out from *Sand Captain,* and Charles Dziuba, in another small boat from McCarthy's marina, together rescued nearly every passenger who escaped death. Within a few minutes, all had been saved who could be, many of them hurt. Twenty injured were dispatched to hospitals.

In the meantime, the first excited radio and television bulletins had gone out on the air. So many curious thousands converged on approaches to the bridge by land and by water that salvage operations became seriously handicapped. The rescue forces soon mobilized sixteen Coast Guard vessels of varying sizes, along with tugboats, fireboats, police launches, and three helicopters. Red Cross, Salvation Army, and civil-defense workers poured into the area. Many police and amateur skin-divers as-

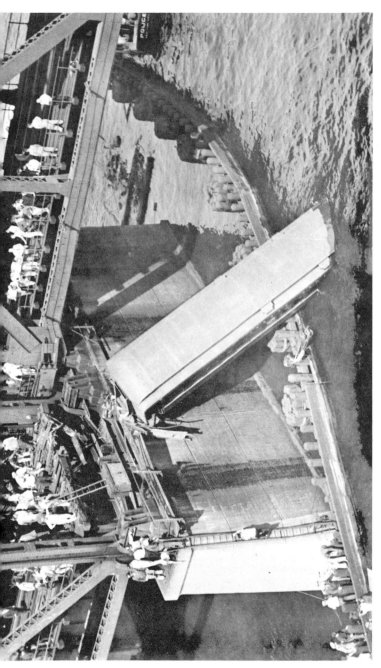

The partly sunken third coach of the Jersey Central's wrecked commuter Train No. 3314 is shown supported by pilings and a pier of the Bayonne lift-bridge after the front end of the train had plunged through the open draw on September 15, 1958. The lift-bridge operated in two halves, one of which has been lowered here to facilitate salvage work and allow partial resumption of railroad traffic.

sembled, but the police allowed only one to dive, for fear of the treacherous currents.

At 9:57 A.M. on that day, the Central Railroad of New Jersey's commuter Train No. 3314, inbound for Jersey City from Bay Head, on the coast, had pulled out of Elizabethport on schedule and headed eastward across the mile-and-a-half-long trestle spanning the busy entrance to the Port of Newark. The train was made up of two 1,500-hp General Motors diesel locomotives and five aging coaches. The second locomotive and the first coach were riding back empty from Bay Head. Most passengers had taken seats in the second, third, and fourth coaches. The last car contained only a mail crew.

On an ordinary Monday, this train carried one hundred passengers or more, many of them New York executives who didn't have to be at their offices until midmorning. There were fewer persons than usual aboard today, because it was Rosh Hashanah, the Jewish New Year.

At 9:57 the train's stocky, sixty-three-year-old engineer, Lloyd Wilburn, a veteran railroader, waved at a signal-tower operator from his open window on the right side of the leading locomotive's cab as No. 3314 gathered speed for its dead-straight run to Bayonne along the southernmost track of the trestle. Wilburn's companion in the cab was Fireman Peter Andrew, forty-two years old, who had had experience as an engineer.

The cab was laid out so that the engineer and fireman could see and hear each other at all times. On that fact was based a safety routine mandatory on the Jersey Central, among many other lines: the engineer would call out each signal as it appeared ahead; the fireman would check the sighting and confirm it in a loud voice. This procedure, officials of the railroad later declared, was believed to be every bit as dependable a safety precaution as the fifty-year-old "dead man's control," a switch that automatically stops a train if the engineer's hand drops from the throttle. Some Jersey Central locomotives were equipped with that very commonly used railroad device—but not this particular locomotive.

Engineer Wilburn had had his required physical examination two months earlier, and had been pronounced to be in "excellent health." Fireman Andrew, investigations afterward revealed, was on restricted duty at the time, because of "moderate elevation of blood pressure." There was no indication to the tower operator on that September morning, however, that anything was wrong with either man as No. 3314 rolled by.

The lift-bridge, with its twin 150-foot draws, carrying a total of four parallel tracks, lay a mile ahead of the moving train. The draws had been raised at 9:55, in preparation for letting *Sand Captain* pass under them on her way to sea.

That bridge had long been a nuisance to the Jersey Central. As Newark's ship traffic grew in volume, the draws were lifted ever more frequently. They were now being raised and lowered more than twenty-five times in an average day. This often interfered with train schedules. The railroad's management had endeavored to persuade ship operators using the Port of Newark to alter their sailing schedules in order to avoid conflict with commuter traffic over the bridge. The effort had met with only small success.

An elaborate system of electrical safeguards had been created for the purpose of preventing the sort of fate that imminently awaited No. 3314.

Three signal lights were spaced along each railroad approach to the bridge. They were located three-quarters of a mile, a quarter of a mile, and 500 feet from the draws. When the bridge was open, the two lights farthest from it shone amber; the third glowed red. Jersey Central rules required a train approaching these signals to start slowing down from a customary 45 mph if the first light was amber, reduce speed to between 15 and 20 mph if the second light was amber, and, of course, stop at the third light if it was red. In the extremely unlikely event that a train should run past all three signals, an automatic derailing device, 50 feet beyond the red light, was set to throw it off the track to the crossties, which presumably would halt it. Signal lights and derailer functioned automatically when the bridge lifted. Conversely, unless the signals and derailer were working properly, the draws could not be opened.

Since the bridge rose normally on this tragic morning at 9:55, its crew could confidently assume that the signals, though they couldn't see them, were working normally, too. The derailer was certainly functioning. A member of the bridge's maintenance crew later testified that he saw the oncoming train leave its rails at that point—at a speed of about 30 mph, he guessed—and bump over the crossties before plunging to its destruction.

Therefore, investigators concluded, the signal lights were also working right.

This piece of knowledge, like almost every other bit of dependable information correlated in the aftermath of the disaster, served only to heighten the mystery of why the wreck occurred.

There was no demonstrable explanation of why Wilburn or Andrew had not responded to the warning signals in time to prevent the accident. Could one of them suddenly have died or become incapacitated? If so, why hadn't the other one stopped the train? Could they *both* have been stricken at the same time? This last possibility was considered too farfetched to countenance.

Although engineer and fireman, for unknown reasons, seemed both to have been entirely oblivious of oncoming catastrophe, at least one passenger on the train saw trouble looming as clearly as did Captain Pederson on the sand dredger. He was Lloyd Nelson, a claims agent for a marine insurance firm. By a coincidence that probably saved his life, Nelson had also been a passenger on the Pennsylvania Railroad train that was derailed at a temporary trestle in Woodbridge, New Jersey, on February 6, 1951. That wreck *(preceding chapter)* was the worst railroad disaster in the history of the metropolitan New York area, but Nelson had escaped from it unhurt. He got away unscathed this time, too, though he might not have done so if his previous experience had not made him more wary than his fellow travelers.

Nelson, riding in the forward portion of the third coach, noted alertly that the lift-bridge was open and that a boat was approaching it from the north. He sensed at once that the bridge could not close in time to allow the fast-moving train to cross it, so he began opening the window beside him. When his car landed headfirst in the water, Nelson was immediately submerged, but he kept his wits about him and hauled himself through the open window. He quickly kicked his way to the surface, where he found a floating hunk of piling and clung to it until pulled into one of the rescue boats in the channel.

Two other men in that third coach had also shared the doleful experience of having been in the 1951 wreck at Woodbridge.

One was a retired but unusually spry professor, seventy-year-old F. Campbell Jeffrey, a former dean of New York Law School. When the car swerved and began pounding over the crossties, other passengers yelled in terror, and Dean Jeffrey thought his last hour had come. Fortunately, he was sitting far enough back in the car so that the flooding water rose only to his waist when the car fell forward and hung steeply from the trestle. There was only one feasible thing to do, and he did it. He pulled himself upward, hand over hand, along the luggage racks and seat backs until he could clamber out onto the firm trestle structure. At any moment, the sharply tilted car might have broken loose and plunged to the bottom, but Dean Jeffrey was too desperately preoccupied to think about that. As it was, he had to boost a faltering fellow passenger to safety before he could gain it himself.

The third passenger who had been in the Woodbridge wreck was Gustave H. Planitz, an insurance broker, who had spent the better part of seven years recovering from the injuries he had previously suffered. Planitz found himself under water when the third car ended its fall, but he escaped by swimming and climbing.

All passengers in the second coach died as it sank in 35 feet of water. Among them were George H. (Snuffy) Stirnweiss, formerly an infielder with the New York Yankees; Elton W. Clark, a director of Allied Chemical Corporation; Mayor John Hawkins of Shrewsbury, New Jersey, a broker carrying $250,000 worth of negotiable securities in his briefcase that morning; and James C. Adams, forty-five, father of four young children, whose wife died of cancer the following day. Hawkins's body was recovered, with the briefcase untouched beside it, when the second coach was raised.

Several women lost their lives, including Mrs. Florence Geogarty, sixty-six-year-old board chairman of a New York firm of customs brokers and freight forwarders; Mrs. Rafael A. Leon, wife of a visiting Venezuelan financier who survived the wreck; and Mrs. Veronica Jurgelowicz, twenty-nine, who died with her four-month-old son in her arms. By a singular turn of fate, Mrs. Jurgelowicz's husband, a Jersey Central electrician just coming off night duty, had ridden past the ill-fated train in the opposite direction on his way home shortly before the accident occurred.

By 3:00 A.M. on September 16th, despite strong tides, a 150-ton floating crane had hoisted the second coach to the surface and lifted it aboard a rail barge containing four tracks. Every window in this coach, which had held more passengers than any other, was found to be broken. The car still retained fifteen bodies, but railroad officials surmised that others had been washed out by the flow of water through the broken windows. Seven bodies had been recovered before this car was raised.

Shortly after midnight on September 17th, the third car, which had been cut loose to fall to the bottom of the channel after salvagers had given up trying to recover corpses from it in its steeply angled position, was hoisted onto the rail barge. It contained four bodies, and a fifth was found hanging from the sling that divers had placed around the car. The divers had already discovered one other body while they were in the act of placing the sling in position.

By midmorning of that day, the first coach, which had been thought to be empty at the time of the wreck, was recovered. A man's body was found caught in the wreckage of the car's roof, which had been staved in, but it was believed to have been carried there from the second or third car by tidal flow.

It was Sunday, September 21st, six days after the wreck, before all forty-eight victims were found and identified. One had been recovered floating off Staten Island, several miles away.

How had this horror come to pass?

Four official investigations of the tragedy began almost immediately after it happened. The Interstate Commerce Commission, the New Jersey Public Utilities Commission, the Army Corps of Engineers, and the Jersey Central all sought to unravel the cruel mystery of why Train No. 3314 hadn't slowed to a stop at the red light 500 feet short of the open bridge.

The tragedy had evolved in the space of 6,000 feet—from the point at which Engineer Wilburn waved to the towerman, to the point at which the train tumbled into Newark Bay—and in the time span of three minutes. Crucial questions concerned the status of the train's mechanical equipment, the functioning of the signal lights, the physical condition of the engineer and fireman both before and during those last three minutes, the varying speeds of the train along the final 6,000 feet of its journey, and the position of the controls in the leading locomotive.

Expert testimony soon brought out the fact that the train's brakes had been checked and found to be working properly just before the fatal run. The signals, too, were reported to have been functioning normally at the time of the accident.

Answers to the remaining key questions came from the bottom of the ship channel, though they by no means solved the principal mystery.

When the leading locomotive was raised, experts found its emergency brakes set, its throttle in a position that would normally have kept the train "barely moving." More thorough investigation subsequently revealed, however, that the brakes had not been applied until the front end of the leading locomotive was *less than eight feet from the open bridge.*

This locomotive, like those of its type, contained a tape that automatically kept a running record of its speed. The tape, when recovered, was found to be somewhat damaged by its long soak in dirty bay water, but the story it told was astonishing. The tape disclosed that at the first signal light the train had slowed either to 8 mph or to a full stop, but had abruptly accelerated to 41 mph, then to 45–46 mph. The last mark on it was a steep up-swing to 58 mph—but the expert testifying, an employee of a firm that manufactured speed recorders for locomotives, said this was doubtless a false reading, caused by the engine's wheels spinning in the air as it fell.

How could one possibly explain the train's seemingly insane rush to disaster?

Medical testimony disclosed that Engineer Wilburn, as was stated earlier, had been declared to be in "excellent health" at the time of his last official physical exam, two months earlier, though his blood pressure had been on a rising curve in recent years. The latest reading, however, had not been considered alarming for a man of his age. Fireman Andrew was on restricted duty, as also has been pointed out, because of moderately elevated blood pressure.

When the bodies of the two men were found and examined, preliminary autopsies had provided conclusions that turned out to be misleading. Wilburn was then thought to have died of a heart attack, Andrew of multiple fractures and bruises.

From these findings, though nothing could be proved, it was reasonable to deduce a scene in which Engineer Wilburn had suddenly died as the train drew abreast of the first signal light, and that in collapsing he had fallen across the throttle, causing the locomotive to surge ahead rapidly. At this, presumably, Fireman Andrew was so shocked that he at first rushed to his friend's aid; then, finding he was beyond help, desperately tried to stop the train by pulling the emergency control. It followed, in this hypothetical explanation, that Andrew died of the injuries he subsequently suffered as the heavy locomotive crashed to the bottom of the channel.

Final autopsy conclusions, announced on October 6th by Dr. Angelo M. Gnassi, chief pathologist of New Jersey's Hudson County, were startlingly different. Wilburn, Dr. Gnassi testified, had not died of a heart attack, but of drowning. He had therefore been alive at the moment the train plunged to its doom. Andrew, on the other hand, though his body had indeed received grave injuries in the subsequent crash, *was already dead before the locomotive hit the water.*

This testimony necessitated a drastic re-staging of the imagined scene in the locomotive cab in the last three minutes before the catastrophe. Presumably, now, Wilburn had had some sort of seizure at the first signal light that temporarily incapacitated him and caused him to lose control of the train. Andrew, it is feasible to assume, was so horrified by this fact and by his instant awareness of the train's acute peril that he suffered a heart attack, a fatal one. Wilburn, struggling to recover, managed at the last instant to release the throttle and pull the emergency control. By then, of course, it was too late.

The truth will never be known. New Jersey's Public Utilities Commissioners, at the conclusion of their hearings on the accident, declared that "unexplained human failure" to obey the warning signals had caused the wreck. One of the saddest ironies pertaining to the Jersey Central disaster was that only after it occurred did the New Jersey Public Utilities Commission order all passenger railroads in that state to install automatic stopping devices—dead-man's controls—on their locomotives.